Fine Motor Projects

W9-BXZ-474

60 Recipes, **50** Activities, and

48 Reproducible Student Pages

Designed to Improve Fine Motor Skills in Young Children

by
Sherrill B. Flora

illustrated by
Julie Anderson

Key Education
An imprint of Carson-Dellosa Publishing LLC
Greensboro, North Carolina

www.keyeducationpublishing.com

CONGRATULATIONS ON YOUR PURCHASE OF A KEY EDUCATION PRODUCT!

The editors at Key Education are former teachers who bring experience, enthusiasm, and quality to each and every product. Thousands of teachers have looked to the staff at Key Education for new and innovative resources to make their work more enjoyable and rewarding. Key Education is committed to developing and publishing educational materials that will assist teachers in building a strong and developmentally appropriate curriculum for young children.

PLAN FOR GREAT TEACHING EXPERIENCES WHEN YOU USE EDUCATIONAL MATERIALS FROM KEY EDUCATION PUBLISHING

Credits
Author: Sherrill B. Flora
Artist: Julie Anderson
Editors: George C. Flora and Karen Seberg
Cover Design: Annette Hollister-Papp
Production: Key Education Staff
Cover Photography: © Comstock
                       © Shutterstock

Key Education
An imprint of Carson-Dellosa Publishing LLC
PO Box 35665
Greensboro, NC 27425 USA
www.keyeducationpublishing.com

Cautions

Before beginning any food activity, ask families' permission and inquire about students' food allergies and religious or other food restrictions.

Before beginning any nature activity, ask families' permission and inquire about students' plant and animal allergies. Remind students not to touch potentially harmful plants during the activity.

Before beginning any outdoor activity, ask families' permission and recommend use of sunscreen and/or sun protection.

Before beginning any scent-related activity, ask families' permission and inquire about students' scent sensitivities and/or allergies.

Before beginning any activity that may cause skin sensitivity, ask families' permission and inquire about students' skin sensitivities and/or allergies.

Printed in the USA • All rights reserved.

ISBN 978-1-60268-118-7
01-335118091

Introduction

Fine motor skills, including grasping, manipulating, and eye-hand coordination, are crucial to early literacy success! Developing the visual discrimination necessary for reading readiness and the manual dexterity needed to write requires concentration and effort—and lots and lots of practice.

Fine Motor Projects provides hundreds of engaging opportunities for children to develop these critical skills. You will find recipes for art materials you can make for and with your children—play dough, colorful chalk, glittery glues, shiny finger paints, and so much more that will inspire imaginations. There are ideas for printing and stamping and reproducible art ready for lacing and stringing. Children can perform finger plays and rhymes using provided puppet patterns. They can also cut, glue, and create with paint, chalk, crayons, and pencils on dozens of delightful ready-to-copy images. Also included to assist your planning are special tips for art experiences, a handy list of inexpensive and readily available materials, and creative ideas for displaying completed art masterpieces.

So, as your students are busy making and creating with the materials and experiencing the fun activities offered in *Fine Motor Projects*, they are also building an important foundation for learning to read and write.

Contents

Readily Available Materials

alum (powdered)
baby lotion
baby shampoo
baking cup paper liners
baking soda
balsa wood
blender
boric acid
bucket
butcher paper
buttermilk
buttons
cake pan (9" x 13")
candy molds
cardboard
card stock
cheese grater
chalkboard paint
chocolate (semisweet)
cinnamon
cloth
clothespins
cloves (ground)
colored chalk
construction paper
contact paper
cookie cutters
cookie sheet
cooking spray
cooling rack
cornmeal
cornstarch
corn syrup
cotton balls
cotton swabs
craft foam
craft sticks
crayons

cream of tartar
dish washing liquid
dry starch
duct tape
eggshells
electric mixer
empty containers
    (baby food,
    coffee cans,
    margarine,
    yogurt)
envelopes
eyedroppers
file folders
film containers
finger paint paper
flavored gelatin
flour
food coloring
fruit baskets
glitter
honey
ice cube trays
instant coffee
instant pudding
liquid starch
liquid tempera paint
iron
ironing board
juices
margarine
markers
masking tape
mixing bowls
muffin pan
newspaper
newsprint
nutmeg

oatmeal
oil of cloves
old catalogs
old magazines
paintbrushes
paper cups
paper plates
paper punch
paper towels
pasta (uncooked)
peanut butter
pencils
pencil sharpener
peppermint oil
pie pans
plaster of paris
plastic lids
plastic utensils
powdered drink mix
powdered milk
powdered sugar
powdered tempera
    paint
rolled oats
rubbing alcohol
salt
saltshaker
sand
sandpaper
saucepan
scissors
seeds
sequins
self-sealing plastic bags
self-stick corkboard
    squares
socks
sponges

spoons
spray bottles
squeeze bottles
straws (plastic)
string
sugar
sugar-free
    powdered gelatin
tacky glue
tape
tin cans
tissue paper
toilet paper tubes
tongue depressors
twigs
vanilla
vegetable oil
vinyl tablecloths
wallpaper samples
waxed paper
wheat flour
white glue
yarn
yogurt (plain)

Special Tips & Ideas
for Presenting Art Experiences to Young Children

✎ **ALWAYS supervise art experiences. Use caution** before beginning any food activity. Ask parents' permission and inquire about children's food allergies and religious or other food restrictions. Even nontoxic art materials can cause problems. Do not let children taste anything unless you know for sure that it is safe! For additional activity cautions, please see page 2.

✎ **ALWAYS** sit with your children and enjoy the experience with them.

✎ Art is a time for exploration and discovery. Do not be surprised if your little ones decide to use the art materials in ways that you did not consider.

✎ Spray a cooking spray on the inside of glue cap tips. This will help to prevent clogging.

✎ Inexpensive vinyl tablecloths are good to keep on hand for messy projects.

✎ Before children can learn to print, they need to develop their fine motor skills and increase their eye-hand coordination. Lacing cards and stringing beads are specific activities designed to promote this development.

✎ Tape the bottoms of new crayon boxes so that the bottom flaps will not fall open.

✎ An old shower curtain on the floor or table is great for catching spills.

✎ Add a few drops of dish washing liquid to any tempera paint. This will make cleanup easier.

✎ Cover an entire tabletop with butcher paper and let your little ones enjoy coloring over the whole table!

✎ Read aloud a favorite story or play a commercially recorded story while the children are "creating art."

✎ Play classical music when your children are busy creating. Research indicates that children who are exposed to classical music have a better chance of obtaining higher math and science scores when they reach school.

Special Tips & Ideas (cont.)

✎ Save yogurt cups to serve as disposable paint containers.

✎ Children can create their own private art galleries with self-stick corkboard squares, which can be found at many home improvement stores. The squares can be placed on any wall or surface. Children will be able to arrange and rearrange their artwork in these cork squares.

✎ Home improvement or paint stores now carry "chalkboard paint." Chalkboard paint can be applied to any wall, at the appropriate height for a child, and creates a surface that is easily washed. How fun for children to be able to write on a wall and not get into trouble!

✎ Children love to paint. Here are some interesting items that can be used as alternatives to paintbrushes:

- ❖ bark
- ❖ brushes
- ❖ chenille craft stems
- ❖ combs
- ❖ cotton balls
- ❖ cotton swabs
- ❖ dandelion blooms

- ❖ eyedroppers
- ❖ feathers
- ❖ flyswatters
- ❖ food
- ❖ ice
- ❖ marbles
- ❖ roll-on deodorant bottles

- ❖ shoe polish applicators
- ❖ sponges
- ❖ spoons and forks
- ❖ spray bottles
- ❖ squeeze bottles
- ❖ string
- ❖ toy wheeled vehicles

✎ **ALWAYS REMEMBER** that with young children, the importance of the art experience is in the process, not in the final product.

Metric Conversions
If you prefer metric measurements, the art recipes in this book can be easily adapted by making a few simple conversions:

1/4 teaspoon = 1.23 mL	1/4 cup = 59.15 mL	1/2 inch = 1.27 cm	200°F = 93°C
1/2 teaspoon = 2.46 mL	1/3 cup = 78.86 mL	1 inch = 2.54 cm	250°F = 121°C
1 teaspoon = 4.93 mL	1/2 cup = 118.29 mL	6 inches = 15.24 cm	300°F = 149°C
2 teaspoons = 9.86 mL	2/3 cup = 157.73 mL	1 foot = 30.48 cm	325°F = 163°C
1/2 tablespoon = 7.39 mL	3/4 cup = 177.44 mL		350°F = 177°C
3/4 tablespoon = 11.09 mL	1 cup = 236.59 mL		400°F = 204°C
1 tablespoon = 14.79 mL	2 cups = 473.18 mL		
2 tablespoons = 29.57 mL	3 cups = 709.76 mL		
1 fluid ounce = 29.57 mL			

8 1/2" x 11" paper = 21.59 cm x 27.94 cm paper
9" x 13" pan = 22.86 cm x 33.02 cm pan

Chapter One
Play Dough

Classroom Tips: Strengthening Hands, Wrists & Fingers

Play dough is always fun for young children to play with, and it is an excellent tool to help build and develop hand strength as well as manual dexterity. The following simple activities will be enjoyed by your children and will help them to further develop their fine motor skills.

• **Pretend you are baking cookies.** Flatten the dough with a rolling pin and use cookie cutters to create shapes. Plastic lids, plastic cups, and plastic silverware may also be used for cutting and making shapes with the play dough.

• **Roll and cut play dough.** Roll the play dough in long, thin, snakelike shapes. Cut the play dough snakes with scissors.

• **Use a variety of kitchen tools.** Squeeze play dough through a potato ricer or garlic press or push it through a funnel. Plastic forks, spoons, and knives can be used to cut play dough and to create impressions, textures, and designs. Use a rolling pin or play with a melon baller or ice cream scoop.

• **Make new play dough colors.** Place two small balls of play dough, each a different color, in a small plastic bag. Push and squeeze the play dough until it is one color. For example, combining a yellow ball of play dough with a blue ball of play dough will create green play dough.

Children love to help make their own play dough. The following recipes have been successfully tried and tested in classrooms and have inspired hours of creative play.

Basic Play Dough Recipe

The Best Basic Play Dough

You will need: **(LARGE BATCH)**

3 cups flour	3 cups water
1 1/2 cups salt	food coloring
3 tablespoons cream of tartar	
3 tablespoons vegetable oil	

(SMALL BATCH)

1 cup flour	1 cup water
1/2 cup salt	food coloring
1 tablespoon cream of tartar	
3/4 tablespoon vegetable oil	

(BOTH) saucepan
spoon or utensil for stirring
large, resealable plastic bag

What you do:

Stir the food coloring into the water in a saucepan. Add the flour, salt, cream of tartar, and vegetable oil to the colored water and mix well. Cook over low heat, stirring constantly, until the dough is no longer sticky. Cool, place it in the plastic bag, and seal it tightly. Knead the dough in the plastic bag for several minutes and then store it in the refrigerator.

The Most Popular Play Dough Recipes

No-Cook Baker's Clay

You will need:
4 cups flour   2 cups water   mixing bowl
1 cup salt   food coloring   spoon or utensil for stirring
1 teaspoon powdered alum

What you do:

Mix the flour, salt, and powdered alum together. Slowly mix the water into the flour mixture, and then knead for several minutes. Divide the dough into smaller balls and add a different color of food coloring to each section of dough. Store in airtight containers. Optional: This dough can also be baked. Use cookie cutters or create your own shapes. Place pieces of dough on an ungreased cookie sheet and bake for 30 minutes in an oven set at 250°F. Turn the pieces over and bake another 30 minutes.

Special tip: For great fine motor practice, "hide" small objects in balls of play dough for children to find.

Great Play Clay

You will need:
1 cup cornstarch   liquid tempera paint or food coloring
2 cups baking soda   microwave-safe bowl or saucepan
1 1/4 cups water   mixing bowl and spoon or utensil for stirring

What you do:

Mix the cornstarch and baking soda together in the mixing bowl. In a microwave-safe bowl, mix the water with the paint or food coloring. Slowly add the cornstarch mixture to the water and stir. Microwave the mixture for several minutes, stopping to stir every 30 to 40 seconds, or cook on the stove over a low heat for approximately 15 to 20 minutes while stirring constantly. This play dough will harden if air-dried and may be painted.

Special tip: Add vanilla extract to any homemade play dough recipe to help prevent mold, preserve the dough, and make the dough smell great!

Play Dough Handprints

You will need:
1 cup flour   2 tablespoons vegetable oil
1/2 cup salt   food coloring
1 tablespoon cream of tartar   mixing bowl and spoon or utensil for stirring
1 cup water   saucepan

What you do:

Combine the flour, salt, and cream of tartar in the mixing bowl. Mix the water, vegetable oil, and food coloring in a saucepan. Bring the liquid mixture almost to a boil. Remove the pan from the heat and add the dry ingredients. Mix well. When the dough is cool, knead for several minutes. Roll the dough into a ball and press it into a circle or oval about an inch thick. Have a child spread her fingers and press her hand into the clay so that it leaves a clear impression. Bake at 200°F for approximately 30 minutes or until the dough hardens. The baking time may vary depending on the size and thickness of the dough circle.

Special tip: Poke a hole in the top of the dough circle with a plastic straw so that the creation can be hung for display.

 # Easy-to-Make Natural Play Dough Recipes

Natural Play Dough

You will need:
1 cup flour
1/2 cup salt
1 tablespoon vegetable oil
2 tablespoons cream of tartar

1 cup water
saucepan and mixing bowls
spoon or utensil for stirring
fruit and vegetable juices

What you do:

   Mix the flour, salt, oil, and cream of tartar together in a saucepan, and then slowly add the water. Cook over a medium heat while stirring constantly until the dough forms a ball and becomes stiff. Divide the dough into three or four balls. Add one of the following fruit or vegetable juices to each ball of dough: grape, carrot, beet, spinach, or orange. The juices will provide the color for the play dough as well as add a wonderful aroma.

Uncooked Oatmeal Play Dough

You will need:
1 cup flour
2 cups oatmeal
1 cup water

mixing bowl
spoon or utensil for stirring

What you do:

   Combine the flour and oatmeal in a mixing bowl. While stirring, gradually add the water. Knead the stiff dough until it is smooth and pliable.

Special tip: Add ground coffee to the play dough to provide another interesting texture.

Tasteable Oatmeal Play Dough

You will need:
2 cups creamy peanut butter
2 cups rolled oats or oatmeal
2 cups powdered milk
2/3 cup honey

food coloring
large mixing bowl
spoon or utensil for stirring

What you do:

   Mix all of the ingredients together in the mixing bowl. Stir and then knead until they reach the consistency of play dough. This fun dough can be tasted, but tasting is recommended only in very small samples.

Option: For older children, add other fun foods to the tasteable oatmeal play dough, such as mini chocolate chips, various colorful cereal pieces, or tiny hard candies.

More Easy-to-Make Natural Play Dough Recipes

Cornmeal Play Dough

You will need:
1 1/2 cups flour
1 1/2 cups cornmeal
1 cup salt
1 cup water

food coloring
mixing bowl
spoon or utensil for stirring

What you do:

Combine the flour, cornmeal, and salt in the mixing bowl. Add the food coloring to the water and then stir it into the flour mixture. Knead the dough until it is easy to manipulate. This play dough has an interesting texture and is fun to squish!

Easy, Edible Peanut Butter Play Dough

You will need:
1 cup creamy peanut butter
1 cup light corn syrup
1 cup powdered sugar

3 cups powdered milk
mixing bowl
spoon or utensil for stirring

What you do:

Mix together the peanut butter, corn syrup, and powdered sugar. Gradually stir in the powdered milk. Knead all of the ingredients together until you have a smooth dough ready for some smooth, yummy fun!

Fun-to-Touch Peanut Butter Play Dough

You will need:
1 cup creamy peanut butter
1 cup honey
1 cup powdered milk

1 cup rolled oats
mixing bowl
spoon or utensil for stirring

What you do:

Put all of the ingredients in the bowl and mix thoroughly. This peanut butter play dough recipe has a grainier texture than the Easy, Edible Peanut Butter Play Dough above.

Option: For extra fun, add raisins, butterscotch and chocolate chips, hard candies, dried fruit, nuts, or pretzels to the peanut butter play dough. Or, make sculptures and use the "mix-ins" to create faces or other features.

Spicy Play Dough Recipes

Spicy Play Dough

You will need:
3 tablespoons nutmeg
2 tablespoons ground cloves
3/4 cup cinnamon
1 cup applesauce

mixing bowl
spoon or utensil for stirring
rolling pin and cookie cutters
waxed paper

What you do:

Mix all of the ingredients together in a mixing bowl. Give children the fun of adding the ingredients and stirring them together. Use a rolling pin to roll out the dough and have children cut out different shapes with cookie cutters. Poke a hole in the top of each shape so that they can be hung. Place all of the shapes on the waxed paper, cover them with another sheet of waxed paper, and let them dry for several days. Be sure to turn the shapes so that they dry evenly.

Cinnamon Play Dough

You will need:
1 cup salt
2 cups whole wheat flour
5 teaspoons cinnamon
1 cup warm water
2 tablespoons vegetable oil
food coloring
2 mixing bowls
spoon or utensil for stirring

What you do:

Combine all of the dry ingredients in a mixing bowl. In another bowl, mix together the water, vegetable oil, and food coloring. Add the flour mixture gradually to the water mixture until the dough reaches the desired consistency. Stir it until it forms a ball. Knead the dough until it is smooth.

Gingerbread Play Dough

You will need:
variety of spices (cinnamon, nutmeg, ginger, allspice)
1 cup flour
1/2 cup salt
2 teaspoons cream of tartar

1 cup warm water
1 teaspoon vegetable oil
2 mixing bowls
saucepan
spoon or utensil for stirring

What you do:

In a mixing bowl, combine enough of the spices to achieve the desired color and scent; then, add them to the remaining dry ingredients in the saucepan. In another bowl, mix together the water and vegetable oil. Add the water mixture to the flour mixture; cook and stir for about 2 minutes. When the dough begins to stick together and pull away from the sides, remove it from the pan, cool slightly, and knead it until it is smooth.

Sweet & Smelly
Play Dough Recipes

Juicy Fruit Play Dough

You will need:
2 cups flour
1 cup salt
4 tablespoons cream of tartar
3-ounce package of sugar-free gelatin
1 cup water

2 tablespoons vegetable oil
mixing bowl
spoon or utensil for stirring
saucepan
waxed paper

What you do:
Stir all of the dry ingredients together in a mixing bowl. Bring the water and oil to a boil in the saucepan and then add the dry ingredients. Reduce the heat to low and stir until the mixture forms a ball. Place on a piece of waxed paper to cool. Children will enjoy the great-smelling play dough fun!

Chewy Chocolate Play Dough

You will need:
10 ounces of semisweet chocolate
1/3 cup light corn syrup
double boiler

mixing bowl
spoon or utensil for stirring
waxed paper

What you do:
Chop the chocolate into small pieces and melt it in the double boiler. Pour the corn syrup into the melted chocolate and stir. Pour the mixture onto waxed paper and spread it around evenly; then, cover the mixture with another sheet of waxed paper. The chocolate play dough will begin to thicken within a couple of hours, but it is best to let it sit overnight. The next day, it will be pliable and can be molded just like real play dough.

Semisweet Chocolate Play Dough

You will need:
1 1/4 cups flour
1/2 cup cocoa powder
1/2 tablespoon cream of tartar
1 cup water

1 1/2 tablespoons vegetable oil
mixing bowl
spoon or utensil for stirring
saucepan

What you do:
Stir all of the dry ingredients together in a mixing bowl. Bring the water and oil to a boil in the saucepan and then add it to the dry mixture. Stir quickly and mix well. When the dough cools, use your hands to finish mixing. Store the dough in an airtight container.

Sweet, Smelly & Sparkling Play Dough Recipes

Sparkling Play Dough

You will need:
- 1 cup flour
- 1 cup water
- 1/2 cup salt
- 1 tablespoon vegetable oil
- 2 teaspoons cream of tartar
- food coloring
- glitter
- saucepan
- spoon or utensil for stirring

What you do:

Mix all of the ingredients together in a saucepan over a medium-low heat. Keep stirring until the dough forms a ball. Remove the dough from the pan and cool. Add glitter to the dough and knead until smooth. This is one play dough recipe that should NOT be refrigerated. When stored in an airtight container, the dough will last for several weeks at room temperature.

Yummy Candy Play Dough

You will need:
- 1/3 cup margarine
- 1/3 cup light corn syrup
- 1 teaspoon vanilla
- food coloring
- 16 ounces of powdered sugar
- mixing bowl
- spoon or utensil for stirring

What you do:

Mix together the margarine, light corn syrup, vanilla, and food coloring. Gradually stir in the powdered sugar. Knead until smooth. It's all right for children to have a taste as they mold this fun dough!

Cool Coffee Play Dough

You will need:
- 1/4 cup instant coffee
- 1 1/2 cups warm water
- 4 cups flour
- 1 cup salt
- 2 mixing bowls
- spoon or utensil for stirring

What you do:

Dissolve the instant coffee in the warm water in one bowl and set it aside. In another bowl, mix the flour and salt. Use a spoon to make a hole in the center of the flour-and-salt mixture. Pour the coffee into the hole, stir it with a spoon, and then knead it with your hands. This play dough should be very smooth. It can also be hardened by baking. Have children make shapes from the dough and place them on a cookie sheet. Bake the shapes at 300°F for 60 minutes.

Snowy Play Dough Recipes

Fluffy Snow Play Dough

You will need:
food coloring   mixing bowl
3 cups warm water   electric mixer
1 cup soap flakes   spoon or utensil for stirring

What you do:

First, add the food coloring to the water. Then, add the soap flakes and beat with an electric mixer until the soap is fluffy and can be manipulated. If you want to pretend that this is "real" snow, do not use the food coloring and simply leave the play dough snow-white.

Cotton Snowball Dough Fun

You will need:
1 cup flour
1 cup water
mixing bowl
spoon or utensil for stirring
cotton balls

What you do:

Mix the flour and water together to form a paste. If the paste mixture is too watery, gradually add a little more flour. Add small amounts of water if the paste is too stiff. Dip the cotton balls into the paste mixture and use them to mold a sculpture. Bake the sculptures for about 60 minutes at 325°F until they become light brown in color. After the sculptures are cool, they can be painted.

Sparkling Snow Dough

You will need:
1 cup flour   silver glitter
1 cup water   1/4 cup white tempera paint
1/2 cup salt   saucepan
2 tablespoons vegetable oil   spoon or utensil for stirring
1 tablespoon cream of tartar

What you do:

Mix all of the ingredients in the saucepan. Stir constantly over medium heat until the mixture forms a ball. When the mixture cools, knead it with your hands. Store it in an airtight container.

Sandy
Play Dough Recipes

No-Cook Super Sand Play Dough

You will need: 4 cups of clean play sand   1 cup water
3 cups flour   mixing bowl
1/4 cup vegetable oil

What you do:
Combine the sand, flour, oil, and water in a mixing bowl. Knead with your hands until the mixture forms a ball. If the mixture is too dry, gradually add water until it reaches a nice dough consistency. If the mixture is too watery, gradually add more flour. This is a super play dough for children who really enjoy tactile experiences.

Special tip: After sculpted objects have dried completely, clear nail polish can be used as a varnish.

Sensational Sand Castle Clay

You will need: 2 cups sand   saucepan
1 cup water   spoon or utensil for stirring
1 cup cornstarch

What you do:
Mix all of the ingredients in a saucepan and cook over a low heat until the mixture is thick and clay like. Let children mold their own visions of a sand castle or sand fort!

Sand-Casting Handprints

You will need: sand   plaster of paris
spray bottle filled with water   water
bucket   mixing bowl
spoon or utensil for stirring

What you do:
Fill the bucket with damp sand. Use the spray bottle filled with water to keep the sand moist. Have a child spread his fingers and press his hand into the center of the sand, making a clean impression with at least an inch of sand all of the way around it. Mix the plaster of paris with water until it is the consistency of whipped cream. Pour the plaster into the impression of the hand, completely filling it. Let it dry overnight; then, lift the plaster out and brush off the sand. Children may also enjoy painting their plaster hand castings with tempera paint. You may wish to spray the hand castings with a clear varnish.

Option: Children enjoy making sand castings. Make impressions in the sand with shells, toys, rocks, buttons, marbles, and other objects to fill with plaster.

Caution: Be sure to read and follow all safety instructions on the plaster of paris label.

"Goopy Stuff" Recipes

Rubbery Goop

You will need: 2 cups baking soda   saucepan
1 1/2 cups water   spoon or utensil
1 cup cornstarch   for stirring

What you do:

Place all of the ingredients in a saucepan over medium heat and stir until smooth. Bring the mixture to a boil and stir it constantly until it is thick. Remove from the heat and cool. Children will enjoy the feel and texture, as well as the movement, of this rubbery goop!

Slimy Goop

You will need: 1/2 cup white glue   wooden spoon
1/4 cup liquid starch   mixing bowl
food coloring (optional)

What you do:

Place all of the ingredients in a bowl and mix with a wooden spoon, craft stick, or tongue depressor. Children will find the goop sticky, yet smooth, and have a lot of "goopy" fun!

Directions for Rolled Play Dough Alphabet Letters (pages 19–21)

Copy and laminate the Rolled Play Dough Alphabet Letter patterns, pages 19–21. You may wish to enlarge the pages or isolate specific letters that children are learning.

Begin with small balls of basic play dough. Help children roll their balls of dough on a smooth surface to create thin ropes. These can be cut with scissors or pinched off into workable lengths of about six inches. Have children position the dough ropes on top of their chosen letters, following the lines and curves. They can reroll the dough to form new letters or save their letters to create words. They will especially enjoy making the letters to form their names!

Special tips:

Follow the recipe's directions to let the letters harden or bake them to create a permanent alphabet for each child. Use a variety of colors of dough for fun or to enhance learning. For example, children can use the same color to make both the upper- and lowercase forms of a letter. Children can also use several sets of dough letters to spell simple CVC words and discover letter patterns. By changing the initial consonant in a word, they will begin to recognize word families, an important first step in learning to read.

(Directions are found on page 18.)

Rolled Play Dough Alphabet Letters

(Directions are found on page 18.)

Rolled Play Dough Alphabet Letters

(Directions are found on page 18.)

Rolled Play Dough Alphabet Letters

Chapter Two

Printing & Stamping

Classroom Tips

Printing and stamping activities are not only fun for children, these projects will strengthen their hand, wrist, and finger muscles and increase their coordination skills.

Build a Classroom Stamp Collection

"Scrapbooking" and the craft of stamping have become popular hobbies. Ask the parents of your students to donate stamps they are no longer using. You may be surprised with how many stamps you receive!

Make Your Own Stamps

You will need: wooden blocks
foam letters, numbers, or shapes (optional: self-adhesive)
glue

What you do:

Save old wooden blocks. Cut out reversed shapes, letters, or numbers from craft foam, self-adhesive shoe liners, or foam self-adhesive mounting tape. Glue the foam shapes to the surfaces of the wooden blocks or peal the backing paper from the self-adhesive shapes and simply stick them to the wooden blocks.

This is an inexpensive way to create stamps for young children. Wooden blocks are easy for small hands to hold and control. Use commercially purchased washable stamping ink pads or make tempera paint pads (see below).

Printing & Stamping Activities

Shape Prints

You will need: smooth and corrugated cardboard   paper plates
glue   tempera paint pad (see below)
paper

What you do:

Collect pieces of smooth and corrugated cardboard of the same thickness. Help children cut the cardboard pieces into small shapes. Glue shapes to the backs of paper plates, using both corrugated and smooth cardboard. Set out a paint pad and paper. Show children how to press the backs of their paper plates onto the paint pad and then onto sheets of paper to make prints.

To make a paint pad:

Make a paint pad by placing a sponge or folded paper towel on a plate and pouring a small amount of tempera paint on it.

Printing & Stamping Activities (cont.)

Food Stamps

You will need: variety of foods (suggestions below)
tempera paint pad (see page 22)
paper

What you do:

Cut the food (apples and potatoes work well for carving) in half. Draw a shape on the flat cut side and then carve around the shape so that it is raised. Press the shape on the paint pad and then stamp it on paper. Marshmallows and cut carrots and cucumbers make great stamps for dabbing pictures made entirely out of circles—similar to the art of pointillism. Other fun foods for stamping include halved green peppers, star fruit, oranges, and mushrooms. Reproduce page 24 and let the children print food shapes in the basket.

Nature Printing

You will need: tempera paint   paper
various objects from nature   pie pan
    (leaves, flowers, pinecones)

What you do:

Pour tempera paint into the pie pan, just enough to cover the bottom. Lay a nature object, such as a leaf, in the paint and then gently press it onto the paper.

Berry Basket Prints

You will need: berry baskets   paper
tempera paint pad (see page 22)

What you do:

Collect clean, empty berry baskets. Let children press the berry baskets onto the paint pad and then onto sheets of paper to make prints. Encourage children to cover their papers with basket prints. Talk about the shapes made by the lines as the prints are overlapped.

Kitchen Gadget Printing

You will need: variety of kitchen utensils   paper
tempera paint pad (see page 22)

What you do:

You can make wonderful prints with kitchen gadgets and tools such as a potato masher, a spatula, a spaghetti spoon, and a pastry cutter. Give each child a large sheet of paper. Let children choose gadgets to press onto the paint pad and then onto their papers to make prints.

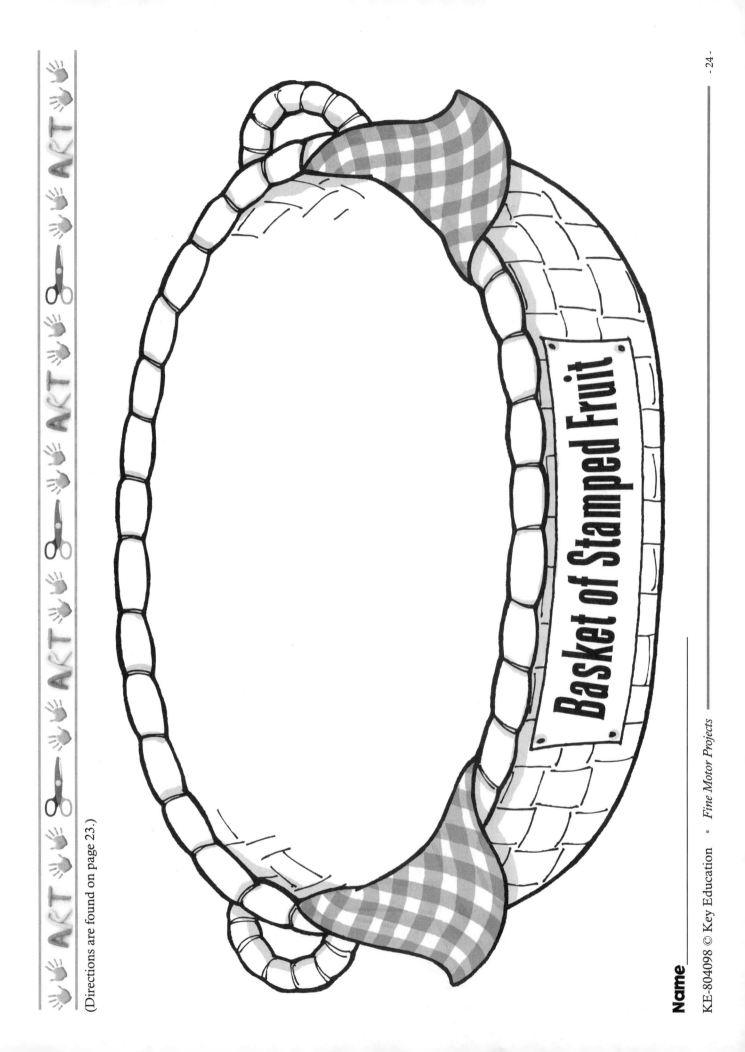

(Directions are found on page 23.)

Basket of Stamped Fruit

Name _____

More Printing & Stamping Activities

Sponge Prints

You will need: pie pans   sponges cut into small squares
liquid tempera paint   spring-type clothespins
  (various colors, including white)   paper (white, blue)

What you do:

Fill the pie pans with a variety of paint colors. Attach a clothespin to each sponge. The clothespin serves as a handle for the sponge and makes it easier for the child to manipulate. Let the children dab paint on the paper. Point out how mixing two colors can create a new color. Reproduce page 26 on blue paper. Let the children sponge white paint on the paper to create a snowman.

Option: Instead of printing with a sponge, use a shower scrunchie for a different texture. Look for other materials or objects that would be fun to use with paint.

Sparkle Prints

You will need: purchased foam stamps   pie pans   glitter
white glue   paper   shoe box

What you do:

Collect two or three foam stamps (simple, solid shapes such as a star, a balloon, or a diamond work best.) Pour a thin layer of glue into a pie pan. Show children how to carefully press one of the foam stamps first into the glue and then onto a sheet of paper to make a print. Let a child make several glue prints. Then, help the child sprinkle glitter all over the glue. (Save the excess glitter by shaking it off into the shoe box.) When the glue has dried, the child will have printed sparkling shapes all over her paper.

Fancy Finger Paint Prints

You will need: finger paint
finger paint paper
white construction paper

What you do:

Tape a piece of finger paint paper on a tabletop. Let children create finger paint masterpieces. Once each painting is finished, press a piece of white construction paper on top of the painting and carefully lift it off. The child will now have a mirror image of the original finger painting.

Option: Have children finger paint on only one-half of their papers. While it is still wet, fold each paper over to create a mirror image print on the other side of the paper.

Stamp-a-Snowman

Chapter Three
Lacing & Stringing Fun

Building fine motor skills and increasing eye-hand coordination are fun for young children when they play with lacing and stringing activities.

Directions for Reproducible Activities

Paper Hole Punch (page 28)

Copy the Good Work Lacing Cards patterns on page 28 onto card stock. Using a paper hole punch is a excellent way to build strength in the hand, wrist, and finger muscles. Let the children have fun using a hole punch to punch out the holes where indicated on the patterns.

Reproducible Lacing Card Patterns (Pages 28–32, 34)

Copy the patterns onto heavy card stock or trace onto cardboard. Color the pictures, laminate for durability, and then punch out the holes where indicated. Children can lace the cards using real shoelaces, curling ribbon, or yarn. Wrap masking tape around one end of the yarn to create a "needle."

Reproducible Stringing Patterns (Pages 33–34)

Copy the patterns onto colored card stock, cut out, laminate for durability, and then punch out the holes where indicated. The children can string the objects using real shoelaces, curling ribbon, or yarn. Wrap masking tape around one end of the yarn to create a "needle."

Homemade Lacing Cards

You will need: coloring books   toy catalogs
discarded children's books   greeting cards

What you do:

Simply glue the pictures onto heavy card stock or cardboard, laminate for durability, and punch holes as desired. Children can lace with shoelaces, ribbon, or yarn.

Colorful Pasta Noodles

You will need: 1/4 cup rubbing alcohol   1 quart self-sealing plastic bag   yarn
1 tablespoon food coloring   paper towels   masking tape
2 cups uncooked pasta shapes

What you do:

To color the pasta, place all of the ingredients in the plastic bag. Shake gently to coat with color. Allow time for the pasta to absorb the color and then spread the pieces on paper towels to dry. Colored pasta shapes such as wheels, penne, and macaroni can provide hours of patterning, beading, and jewelry-making fun. Use a rainbow of colors on many varieties of pasta and place them in a bucket with some yarn or string. Wrap masking tape around the end of the yarn to serve as a needle when stringing the pasta shapes.

Jewelry Making

Special tips: Children will enjoy stringing bracelets and necklaces from a wide variety of materials. Edible necklaces can be made from round cereal pieces and candy. Other kinds of jewelry can be made from small plastic craft beads, buttons, pasta, "figure 8" packing peanuts, drinking straws cut into small pieces, and homemade play dough beads. (Roll the dough into balls, poke a hole through the middle of each bead, and allow them to dry.)

Good Work Lacing Cards

I DID
★ A ★
GREAT
JOB!

GREAT
LISTENER!

Good
Friend
Award!

I
Picked
Up!

(Directions are found on page 27.)

Owl Lacing Card

(Directions are found on page 27.)

Pine Tree Lacing Card

(Directions are found on page 27.)

Heart Lacing Card

(Directions are found on page 27.)

Sun Lacing Card

(Directions are found on page 27.)

Jewelry to String

(Directions are found on page 27.)

Fun Things to Lace & String

— 34 —

Chapter Four

Finger Plays & Puppets

The use of finger plays and finger puppets are effective tools for helping children learn how to control finger movement, increase coordination, and enhance manual dexterity. Children must listen, watch, and practice when learning how to correctly make the finger movements that go with each sentence in a finger play.

Easy-to-Make Puppets

Small Container Finger Puppets

You will need: film containers   craft objects of your choice
glue   (wiggle eyes, felt, yarn, pom-poms)

What you do:
Film containers are easy to balance on fingertips. Turn the containers upside down and add eyes and other facial features. Create film container puppets for the characters in the finger plays you have chosen to share.

Photographic Finger Puppets

You will need: digital camera   photo paper   construction paper
computer and printer   white glue   scissors and tape

What you do:
Using a digital camera and a computer makes it possible to create unique and personal finger puppets. Take and print a photograph, cut out the faces in the photo, and glue each to a strip of construction paper. Loop the construction paper strip around a fingertip and tape it in place.

Lunch Bag Puppets

You will need: paper lunch-size bags   glue
craft objects of your choice   scissors

What you do:
Place the bag flat on a surface with the folded-over bottom of the bag facing up. Use a variety of craft objects to create a face as shown with the mouth overlapping the folded base so that it can open and close.

Paper Plate Puppets

You will need: paper plates   large craft sticks   tape
craft objects of your choice   scissors   glue

What you do:
Let children create puppet faces on paper plates using glue and a variety of craft materials. Tape a large craft stick to each plate to make handles for the puppets.

Easy-to-Make Puppets (cont.)

Finger Puppet Garden Gloves

Use inexpensive garden gloves to create finger puppet gloves. Attach or draw a face on each fingertip. For example, draw the characters in the story "Little Red Riding Hood," including the Wolf, the Woodcutter, Grandmother, and Little Red Riding Hood's Mother. The children can then hold up the correct character as they listen to the tale. It will be well worth your time to make classroom gloves for children to use as you tell traditional stories.

Option 1: Reproduce the face patterns below. Then, color, laminate, and glue them to the fingers of a glove.

Option 2: Children can tell their own stories with individual finger puppets. Simply cut off the fingers of a garden glove. Decorate each finger with craft items or draw facial features with fine point permanent markers.

Little Red Riding Hood	Woodcutter	Little Red Riding Hood's Grandmother	Little Red Riding Hood's Mother

Troll	Biggest Billy Goat	Middle-Sized Billy Goat	Littlest Billy Goat

(Use for "Little Red Riding Hood"
and "The Three Little Pigs")
Wolf

Straw Pig   Sticks Pig   Bricks Pig

Stick & Hand Puppets

Spoon Puppets

Gather plastic spoons in assorted colors and a variety of craft materials, such as stickers, colorful paper, yarn, fabric scraps, and glue. Children can use these to make interesting faces on the bowl of each spoon; they may wish to use fine point permanent markers to add details. Fashioning hair and simple clothes will add to the fun.

Sock Puppets

Have each child slip a sock onto her nondominant hand. Ask her to open her hand so that her thumb and fingers create a mouth. Push the extra sock fabric into the "mouth." Then, with a marker, draw on the sock to indicate where the puppet's eyes, nose, lips, hair, and any other desired features should be placed. Remove the sock and glue a variety of craft materials in position to create a very special character!

Straw Puppets

Children can use photos or pictures of people in magazines or draw faces on sturdy paper. Let them cut out the faces and tape a straw to the back of each.

Envelope Puppets

Seal the flap of the envelope. Then, depending on its size, either slit the bottom or trim one side to the desired width. Place the envelope with the open side down. Children can use markers, felt, craft feathers, small pom-poms, and other craft materials to make puppets of people, animals, or any creature they can imagine.

Puppet Theaters

Appliance Box Theater

Cut a large window in an appliance box so that a child can comfortably kneel while performing his show. Be sure to give every child a chance to "act" as well as be an appreciative member of the audience.

Trifold Display Board Theater

Purchase a foam or cardboard display board and cut a window as shown. Portable and storeable, this mini theater can quickly be set up on a table or desk. It's always ready for spontaneous shows!

Rhymes & Puppet Patterns

Have children dramatize each rhyme as they say it, either using puppets or performing the movements.
Copy the patterns to use as stick puppets or reduce in size to make finger puppets.

TEDDY BEAR, TEDDY BEAR

Teddy bear, teddy bear, turn around.
Teddy bear, teddy bear, touch the ground.
Teddy bear, teddy bear, reach up high.
Teddy bear, teddy bear, touch the sky.
Teddy bear, teddy bear, touch your shoe.
Teddy bear, teddy bear, I love you!
(Perform each action;
end with hands over heart.)

THAT'S ME

This is me, I'd like you to meet
(Bow.)
I have one little head and two little feet.
(Shake head; then shake feet.)
I have two little arms and one little nose,
(Hold up arms; then touch nose.)
And ten little fingers and ten little toes!
(Wiggle fingers and toes.)

WHOO-WHOO

"Whoo-whoo," said the owl,
Sitting in the tree.
(Extend arm like a branch for owl to perch on.)
"During the day,
I'm quiet as can be."
(Put index finger to lips.)

"Whoo-whoo," said the owl,
"I'm awake at night."
(Open eyes wide.)
"I hunt, I eat, *(Move owl to fly.)*
and then sleep when it's light."
(Rest head on touching hands to sleep.)

Rhymes & Puppet Patterns (cont.)

THREE SNOWMEN
Three big snowmen,
Standing in a row.
(Hold up three big snowmen.)
Out came the sun,
And one melted so slow.
(Hold up the semimelted snowman.)

Two big snowmen,
Standing up tall.
*(Hold up two big snowmen
and one melted snowman.)*
The sun kept shining,
Now one is small.
(Hold up the semimelted snowman.)

One big snowman,
He'll be fine, we're told.
*(Hold up one big snowman
and two melted snowmen.)*
The wind outside is very cold!

Make three big snowmen
stick or finger puppets.

Make two melted
snowmen stick or
finger puppets.

Make one semimelted
snowmen stick or
finger puppet.

Rhymes & Puppet Patterns (cont.)

SIX LITTLE DUCKS

Six little ducks went out to play,
Over the hill and far away.
Mother duck said, "Quack, quack, quack,"
And five little ducks came waddling back.

Five little ducks went out to play,
Over the hill and far away.
Mother duck said, "Quack, quack, quack,"
And four little ducks came waddling back.

Four little ducks went out to play,
Over the hill and far away.
Mother duck said, "Quack, quack, quack,"
And three little ducks came waddling back.

Three little ducks went out to play,
Over the hill and far away.
Mother duck said, "Quack, quack, quack,"
And two little ducks came waddling back.

Two little ducks went out to play,
Over the hill and far away.
Mother duck said, "Quack, quack, quack,"
And one little duck came waddling back.

One little duck went out to play,
Over the hill and far away.
Mother duck said, "Quack, quack, quack,"
And no little ducks came waddling back.

Make six little duck stick puppets. Enlarge to make one mother duck. Children may work in groups to dramatize the rhyme.

Or, reduce in size and make six finger puppets for each student.

Chapter Five

Glue & Collage Art

Something as simple as glue can be used for many easy-to-do art experiences and will provide hours of creative fun! With the following activities children can mix, squeeze, sprinkle, tweeze, build, and cut. They will also play with the concepts of color and texture, all while strengthening their fine motor skills.

 # Glue Recipes

Make-Your-Own Colored Glue

You will need: old markers   water   paper
     small bottles of white glue   mixing bowls

What you do:

Don't throw away those old markers! Remove the fiber tubes and let each color soak separately in a bowl of water; take them out when the water starts to turn color. Place the tubes in separate bottles of glue until the glue is colored. The children can use the colorful glue like puff paint, squeezing it to create designs on pieces of paper. They will have fun tracing their fingers over the smooth glue lines when the art is dry.

Option 1: Add glitter to the colored glue for an extra fun effect and added texture. Widen the opening in the glue tip if squeezing the glitter glue or let children apply it with cotton swabs.

Option 2: Children can use the colored glue to write numbers, letters, and names to trace with fingertips.

Puffy Glue

You will need: shaving cream   mixing bowl   paper
     white glue   food coloring   craft sticks or cotton swabs

What you do:

Mix equal parts of shaving cream with glue; add food coloring if you want. Children can use craft sticks or cotton swabs to stir the glue and "paint" it on the paper. The mixture will be puffy when it dries.

Great "Glue" for Kids

You will need: 1 cup flour   pinch of salt   spoon or utensil for stirring
     water   mixing bowl

What you do:

Children can make this gluey paste themselves! In the mixing bowl, help them slowly add water to the flour, stirring constantly. The mixture should be gooey, not drippy. Stir in the salt. Children will love the experience of making their own paste to use for many paper art projects.

Glue Recipes That Smell

Fruity Smells Glue

You will need: instant powdered drink mix   small paper cups   paper or paper plates
white glue   craft sticks   paintbrushes

What you do:

Pour a small amount of white glue into several paper cups. Add some of the drink mix powder to each cup and let children stir it with craft sticks. This activity is even more fun if you use several different flavors of mix. The children can paint the colored, fruity, "flavored" glue onto paper or paper plates. (You may want to make some of the drink mix so that children can taste what they are seeing and smelling.) Let children touch the glue when it is dry. Have them smell their fingers. Does the scent rub onto their fingertips?

Spicy Smells Glue

You will need: various spices (see below)   small paper cups   paper or paper plates
white glue   craft sticks   paintbrushes

What you do:

Follow the directions for Fruity Smells Glue above but instead use spices—cinnamon, onion, garlic, cloves, nutmeg, dill, or anything else you would like to experiment with. You might also try flavorings or extracts such as peppermint or lemon. Let children stir the glue with craft sticks and paint designs on paper.

Option 1: Let the children smell the scents when they are wet and when they are dry. Is there a difference?

Option 2: When the glue is dry, let children play "guess the flavor."

Option 3: Make a graph of which spicy smells the children liked and which ones they did not like.

Glue Activities

Tweezing Seed Pictures

You will need: construction paper   black markers
variety of clean, dry, large seeds   glue

What you do:

Ask children to draw a scribble design with a black marker on a piece of construction paper. Have each child squeeze glue to fill a section of the design. Then, children can use tweezers to place the seeds, such as pumpkin or squash, on the glue. Repeat with another section and a different type of seed. The seed designs are attractive and tweezing seeds is a great exercise for developing fine motor skills.

Make-Your-Own "Glitter" to Shake Over Glue

You will need: 7 to 8 drops of food coloring   1/2 cup salt   mixing bowl and spoon

What you do:

Combine the salt and food coloring in a bowl and stir until the color is evenly distributed. Set the colored salt in the sun to dry or place it in the microwave for 30 to 60 seconds. When the salt is completely dry, it can be stored in a salt shaker and used just like glitter.

Glue & Sticker Activities

Self-Sticking Sticker Ideas

Stickers can provide children with hours of fun and help improve their fine motor skills. Help them create rebus sticker stories; draw a bus and let children fill it with people and animal stickers; make a farm scene to which they can add farm animal stickers; on black construction paper, children can create a space picture with outer space and alien stickers; or provide blue construction paper for children to use fish stickers in an ocean or underwater scene.

The Best Beginning Glue Activity—Paper Chains

Cut 1" x 6" strips of construction paper in a variety of colors. Children can make long paper chains by looping the strips and gluing together the ends. Glue sticks work very well for this activity.

Buildings/Sculptures on Paper

You will need: tacky glue   cardboard or heavy paper
                    small paper cups   cotton swabs
                    craft sticks

What you do:

Pour a small amount of tacky glue into paper cups. Give each child some glue, a piece of cardboard or heavy paper, cotton swabs, and many craft sticks. Have children dip the tips of the cotton swabs into the glue and use them to apply glue to the craft sticks. Children can glue the craft sticks onto the cardboard in any pattern. Five- and six-year-olds might try to use their craft sticks to construct shapes of houses or buildings.

3-D Buildings/Sculptures

You will need: tacky glue   paper plates
                    small paper cups   cotton swabs
                    small wood pieces (balsa)

What you do:

Pour a small amount of tacky glue into paper cups. Give each child a variety of small pieces of wood (balsa wood works well and is easy to manipulate), a paper plate, cotton swabs, and the glue. Using the paper plate as a base, children can use the cotton swabs to apply the glue to their wood pieces, stacking the wood into interesting shapes or three-dimensional forms.

Great Collage Activities

Junk Collage

You will need: white glue   assorted small, fun objects (see below)
construction paper

What you do:
   Collect a variety of small junk objects: old pieces of jewelry, buttons, packing peanuts, old greeting cards, pieces of cardboard, and so on. Craft items, such as jewels, craft feathers, foam shapes, and sequins will add to the fun. Children will love examining the treasures and choosing how to arrange and glue them on construction paper.

Texture Collage

You will need: scissors   small nature objects
white glue   assorted textured papers
construction paper

What you do:
   Provide small objects with interesting textures. If possible, let children take a walk outside to choose their own objects from nature, such as leaves, twigs, bits of bark, or flowers. Also, set out scissors and a variety of textured papers, such as sandpaper, corregated cardboard, and flocked wallpapers. Children will enjoy touching the materials as they create collages on construction paper.

Letter Collage

You will need: scissors   pages from old newspapers,
white glue   magazines, and catalogs
construction paper

What you do:
   Give each child a pair of scissors, glue, and a piece of construction paper. Then, let them page through discarded print media looking for large and/or colorful letters to cut out, arrange into designs, and glue. Although this activity is just for fun, some children may enjoy looking for and choosing specific letters, especially the ones in their names!

Fabric Collage

You will need: white glue   small scraps of fabric (see below)
construction paper

What you do:
   Fabrics are wonderful collage material—the colors, patterns, and textures are a treat for the senses as children arrange and glue pieces into designs. Be sure to have a variety of textiles for children to choose from, such as corduroy, dotted swiss, velvet, satin, burlap, fleece, and fake fur.

Chapter Six
Scissors

Early Learning Tips

Before children can successfully cut with a pair of scissors, they need to develop several different skills. First, they must have enough muscle strength to be able to control and coordinate using two hands together (one hand holds the paper, while the other hand manipulates the scissors). They must also be able to isolate the actions of their thumbs, middle fingers, and index fingers. The ability to separate the movements of these fingers allows children to control the opening and closing of the scissors. Here are some helpful suggestions:

- **Have good scissors.** Make sure you have good pairs of scissors that were designed to fit properly in the children's hands.

- **Practice manual dexterity.** Have children practice touching each fingertip to the thumb. First, touch the pointer finger to the thumb; next, touch the middle finger to the thumb; then, touch the ring finger to the thumb; and finally, touch the pinkie finger to the thumb.

- **Talk about scissor safety.** Discuss the following safety rules prior to giving a child a pair of scissors: You should never run while holding a pair of scissors. You should be sitting when you are cutting with a pair of scissors. If you are walking with scissors, be sure to hold the closed blades in the palm of your hand.

- **Practice opening and closing.** Let the children sit and practice opening and closing the scissors before you give them anything to cut.

- **At first, use heavy paper.** Give children a heavier weight paper when they are first learning to use scissors. Its stability makes it easier to hold and to cut. As a child's skills increase, then introduce lighter weight papers.

- **At first, cut small pieces of paper.** Start with small pieces of paper because they are easier to hold when cutting.

- **Teach "snipping" first.** Let children snip fringe approximately one inch in length along the edge of a piece of paper.

- **Cut lots of different things.** Let children practice cutting using a wide variety of paper and other cuttable things, such as sandpaper, aluminum foil, paint sample squares, waxed paper, yarn, paper straws, play dough, or any other items that you might have handy.

- **Begin with cutting straight lines.** Be sure that young children have mastered cutting straight lines and geometric shapes before introducing the concept of cutting on a curve.

Scissor Activities

Snipping Funny Shapes

You will need: scissors   construction paper
                    contact paper   in a variety of colors

What you do:

Let children enjoy cutting colored construction paper. It does not matter how big or what shapes the pieces are. First, remove the backing on 8.5" x 11" pieces of contact paper. When children have a small pile of colored shapes, they can simply "stick" the shapes on the contact paper, leaving some spaces and the outer edges open. When finished, the contact paper can be turned over and applied to another sheet of paper. The result is a work of scissor art ready for display!

Scissor Cutting Magazines and Catalogs

You will need: scissors
                    old magazines and catalogs

What you do:

This simple activity is very educational and terrific for fine motor development. It is also an activity that children enjoy doing for long periods of time. Simply provide scissors and old magazines or catalogs and let them cut out pictures that interest them.

Special tip: Use the activity to help children learn how to categorize and sort. Have children spread out their pictures and then sort them into specified categories, such as people, furniture, clothing, or food.

Option: Children will also enjoy making collages of pictures of their favorite things. Supply glue sticks and pictures that they have cut out. They can arrange and glue the pictures on pieces of construction paper.

Mosaics

You will need: scissors   white glue   paintbrushes
                    variety of colored tissue paper   clay pot

What you do:

Ask the children to cut many small pieces of colored tissue paper. When they are finished cutting, have them paint their clay pots with diluted white glue. After the pots are covered in glue, children can apply the cutout pieces of tissue paper to their pots. Let the pots dry thoroughly.

Option: Provide each child with a simple coloring book page. Have children use their cut tissue paper pieces to create mosaics. Using glue sticks, children may glue the small pieces of paper in each section to finish their pages.

The Cutting Box

You will need: scissors   large box   paper
                    variety of materials to cut   glue sticks

What you do:

This simple activity will quickly become a classroom favorite. Fill a large box with all sorts of materials that the children can cut. Leave scissors, glue sticks, and paper near the cutting box so that the cut up remnants can be turned into wonderful art projects. The children will love practicing their cutting skills when they know that they can go to a box in which everything is OK to cut!

 **ART**

Directions: Cut out the objects used in school. Glue them in place.

Name: _____

School Tools

(glue here)

(glue here)

(glue here)

(glue here)

Name: _____

Directions: Help build the igloo!
Cut out the blocks of ice.
Glue them in place.

Igloo

(glue here)

(glue here)

(glue here)

(glue here)

Name: _____

Directions: Decorate the tree!
Cut out the ornaments.
Glue them in place.

Tree Ornaments

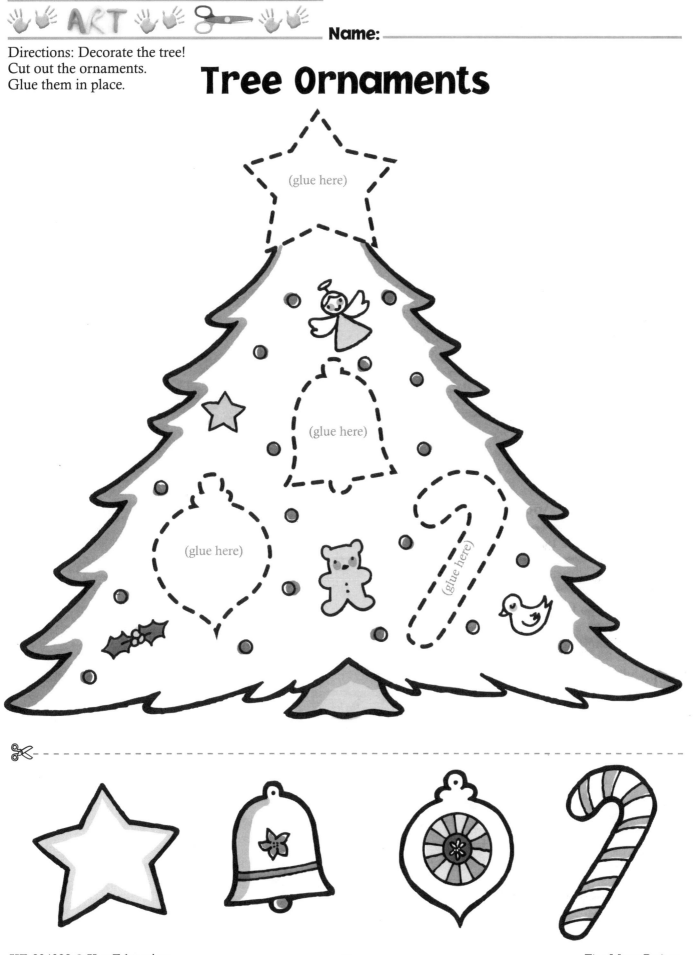

Name: _____

Presents

Directions: Give a gift! Cut out the presents. Glue them in place.

(glue here)

(glue here)

(glue here)

Mittens

Directions: Match the mitten shapes.
Cut out the mittens. Glue them in place.

Name:

(glue here)

(glue here)

Name: _____

Snowman

Directions: Build a snowman!
Cut out the snowballs. Glue them in place.

(glue here)

(glue here)

(glue here)

Directions: Find the pot of gold! Cut out the cloud, sun, and pot. Glue them in place.

The Pot of Gold

(glue here)

(glue here)

(glue here)

Name _____

Name: _____

Directions: Watch the flowers bloom! Cut out the flowers. Glue them on the stems.

Spring Flowers

(glue here)

(glue here)

(glue here)

✂ — — — — — — — — — — — — — — — — — —

 **ART**

Name: _____

Directions: Fill the fishbowl.
Cut out the four fish.
Glue them in place.

Fishbowl

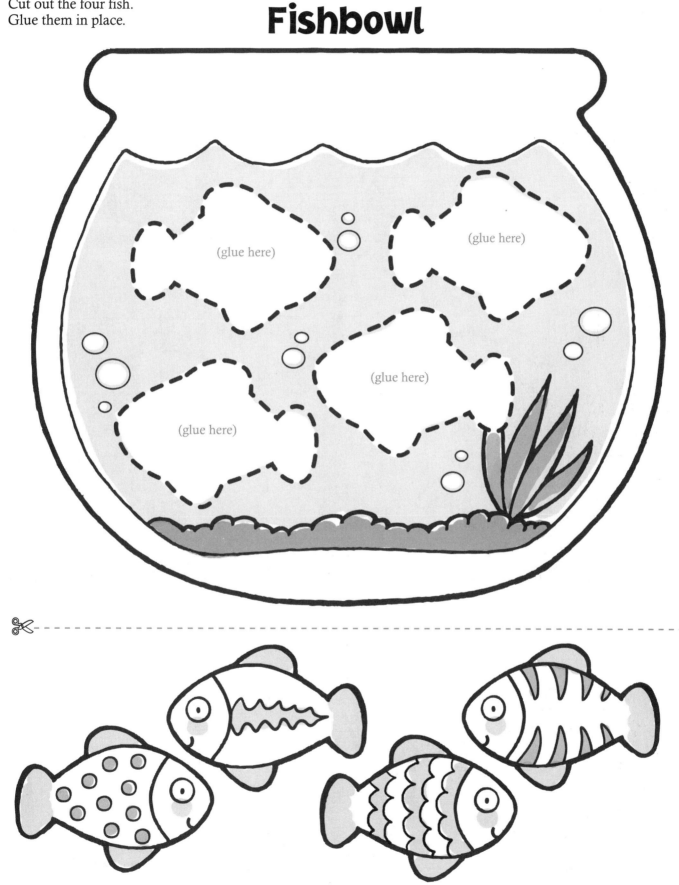

(glue here)

(glue here)

(glue here)

(glue here)

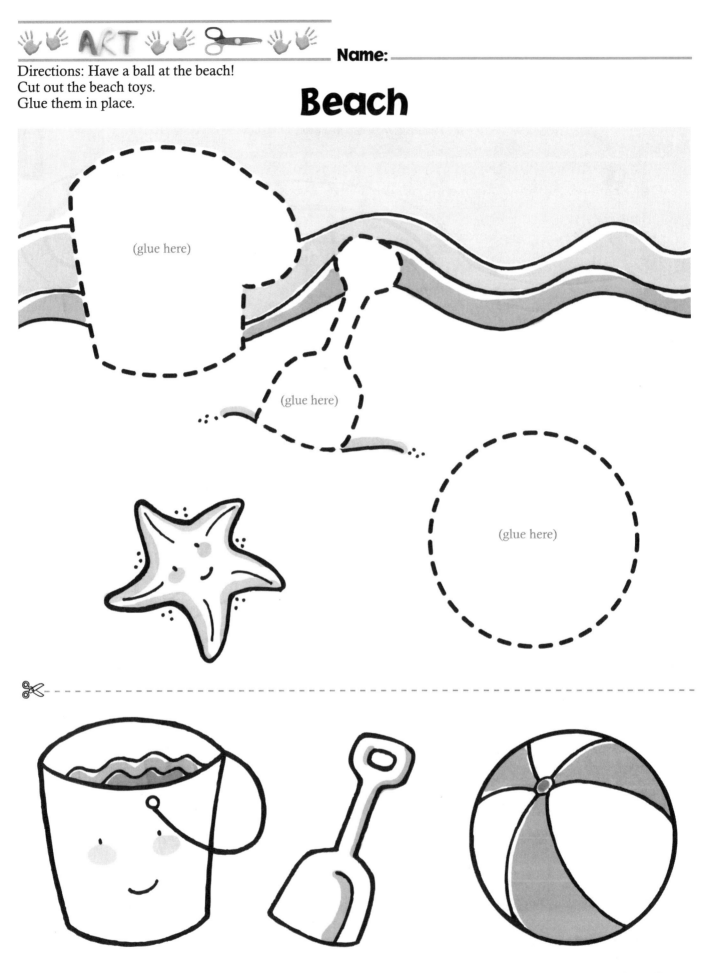

Directions: Have a ball at the beach!
Cut out the beach toys.
Glue them in place.

Name: _____

Beach

(glue here)

(glue here)

(glue here)

Chapter Seven

Painting

Easy Make-Your-Own Paint Recipes

Think back to your childhood—what are your memories of finger painting? Most adults have fond recollections of the experience. Feeling the texture and watching the movement of the paint on the paper is a tremendous sensory experience that also strengthens children's eye-hand coordination and manual dexterity skills. Here are some easy-to-make finger paint recipes that will provide your eager artists with hours of fun!

Recipe 1: Finger Paint Fun

You will need:
    liquid starch   large mixing bowl
    powdered tempera paint   finger paint paper
    spoon or utensil for stirring

What you do:
Simply add the powdered tempera paint to the liquid starch until you have achieved the desired color. That's it! Your children are ready to paint!

Special Tip: Involve children in making this recipe. They will enjoy stirring and benefit from the opportunity to strengthen fine motor skills.

Recipe 2: Finger Paint Fun

You will need:
    2 tablespoons dry starch   saucepan
    6 tablespoons cold water   spoon or utensil for stirring
    1/2 cup boiling water   finger paint paper
    food coloring

What you do:
Dissolve the starch in the cold water. Add this mixture to the boiling water, stirring constantly. Heat the mixture until it becomes glossy. Add the food coloring and stir it well. Let it cool completely before children use it.

Special tip 1: For an easier cleanup, add a small amount of liquid dish washing liquid to the finger paint. Although the cleanup is easier, make sure children still wear a paint smock or an old dress shirt!

Special tip 2: Always make sure that children are finger painting on the shiny side of the paper.

Wonderful Window Finger Paint

You will need:
    liquid tempera paint   tape
    dish washing liquid   newspaper
    containers for the paint   spoon or utensil for stirring

What you do:
Use the tape and newspaper to protect the walls and flooring. Pour the paint into the containers and mix in the dish washing liquid. The dish washing liquid will help to make the paint removal easier. Let children create window masterpieces.

Tasteable Finger Paint Recipes

Wonderful Whipped Cream Creations

You will need: container of whipped topping   spoon or utensil for stirring
food coloring   thick paper or paper plates
large mixing bowl

What you do:

Combine the whipped topping with only a drop or two of food coloring—too much will make the topping runny. Let children "paint" on thick paper or paper plates.

WARNING! Anytime food coloring (or flavored gelatin) is used for colorant, it will stain fingertips, which will eventually come clean. It can also stain clothing and laminated counters. Be careful— but have fun!

Super Sticky Finger Paint

You will need: corn syrup   spoon or utensil for stirring
food coloring   containers for storing paint
mixing bowls   finger paint paper

What you do:

Mix the corn syrup with a drop or two of food coloring. Store a variety of colors in air-tight containers or resealable plastic bags for future use. This finger paint is very sticky, until it dries to an incredible shine.

Instant Pudding Finger Paint

You will need: any flavor of instant pudding   food coloring (for vanilla pudding)
milk   spoon or utensil for stirring
large mixing bowl   paper plates

What you do:

Mix the pudding according to the directions on the box. Let children finger paint with the pudding on paper plates. This is truly yummy art!

Yummy Yogurt Finger Paint

You will need: 1/2 carton plain yogurt   spoon or utensil for stirring
1/2 package flavored gelatin   paper plates or waxed paper
large mixing bowl

What you do:

Mix the gelatin into the yogurt and children are ready to finger paint on paper plates or waxed paper. They will love this "healthy-to-taste" art experience!

Giggly Jiggly Gelatin Finger Paint

You will need: flavored gelatin   spoon or utensil for stirring
9" x 13" pan   finger paint paper

What you do:

Mix the gelatin according to the package directions. Place the gelatin in the refrigerator until it has a gooey consistency! Then, let children use the gelatin to finger paint for some icky–sticky, hilarious fun!

Interesting Make-Your-Own Paint Recipes

Easy Shiny Paint

You will need:
white glue
liquid tempera paint
paper cups

spoons or utensils for stirring
paintbrushes
paper

What you do:
Pour white glue into several paper cups. Add liquid tempera paint to each cup and let children stir until the desired colors are reached. They can use paintbrushes to brush the glossy paint on the paper. As the paint dries, it will not lose its shine. This paint can also be used on wood, paper, and rocks.

Glossy Milk Paint

You will need:
powdered milk
water
powdered tempera paint

large mixing bowls
spoons or utensils for stirring
paper

What you do:
Mix equal parts of water and powdered milk. Add the tempera paint for color and let children stir. This simple paint recipe creates a paint that dries quickly and has an opaque appearance.

Ice Cube Paint

You will need:
ice cube tray
water
food coloring

craft sticks
paper

What you do:
Fill an ice cube tray with water. Add both food coloring and a craft stick to each ice cube section in the tray. Place the tray in the freezer until the colored water is frozen. Provide children with paper and the paint frozen on a stick. They can move the Popsicle-like frozen paint around the paper to "paint."

Option: Let children experiment with ice cube paint on coffee filters.

Frozen Rainbow Paint

You will need:
ice cube tray
liquid tempera paint

craft sticks
paper

What you do:
In an ice cube tray, add a shallow layer of tempera paint and a craft stick to each of the ice cube sections. Place the tray in the freezer until the first layer is almost frozen. Then, add another layer of a different color of paint and so on, until there are four or five layers of paint in each ice cube section. Provide children with paper and cubes of frozen rainbow paint. As children paint and the frozen rainbow paint begins to melt, the colors will become more intense.

Textured & Smelly Finger Paint Recipes

Thick & Minty Finger Paint

You will need:
wallpaper paste or wheat paste
water
food coloring
peppermint oil

large mixing bowl
spoon or utensil for stirring
finger paint paper

What you do:
Mix the wallpaper paste or wheat paste with water to thin it. Add food coloring and a few drops of peppermint oil and mix well. For more fun, make more paint and add other scented oils or extracts, such as lemon, grapefruit, almond, or vanilla.

Clove-Scented Finger Paint

You will need:
2 cups flour
2 cups cold water
1 cup sugar
6 cups boiling water

1 tablespoon boric acid
oil of cloves
food coloring
finger paint paper

large mixing bowl
saucepan
spoon or utensil for stirring

What you do:
Mix the flour and cold water together in the bowl. Add the sugar and stir until smooth. Then, add this mixture to the 6 cups of boiling water in the saucepan, stirring constantly until thick. Remove from the heat and add 1 tablespoon of boric acid and several drops of the oil of cloves. Stir in the food coloring. Store the paint in sealed containers.

Gritty Finger Paint

You will need:
1 cup flour
1 to 1 1/2 cups of salt or sand
1 cup water
food coloring

large mixing bowl
spoon or utensil for stirring
finger paint paper

What you do:
Combine the flour and salt or sand. Add the water and stir until thoroughly mixed. Add the food coloring one drop at a time until you achieve the desired color.

Silky Smooth Finger Paint

You will need:
1 cup water
1/4 cup salt
2 tablespoons cornstarch

food coloring
saucepan
spoon or utensil for stirring

finger paint paper
containers

What you do:
Mix the water, salt, and cornstarch in a pan and bring it to a boil. Keep stirring until the mixture is the consistency of yogurt. If you want to make a variety of colors, divide the mixture, place it in different containers, and add the food coloring. When cool, this mixture will feel smooth and silky.

 # Body & Bath Paint Recipes

These are safe recipes that encourage silly fun. The first recipe creates a soapy body paint. It is highly recommended that you save this art experience for a warm summer day, when the children can wash off the paint as they run through a sprinkler. Although any shampoo, lotion, or bubble bath will work, please use baby products for the following recipes. Baby products have been tested and are known to be gentle for children's skin.

Body Paint for Kids

You will need: baby shampoo   mixing bowls
powdered tempera paint   spoon or utensil for stirring

What you do:
Gradually add the powdered tempera paint directly to the shampoo until you achieve the desired color and consistency. The children will giggle and giggle as they lather their bodies with color. (Remember to have children run through the sprinkler to wash off all of the paint.)

Clown Face Paint

You will need: 1/2 teaspoon powdered tempera paint
1/4 cup baby lotion
dish washing liquid
mixing bowls
spoon or utensil for stirring

What you do:
Mix together the powdered tempera paint with the baby lotion. Add a generous squirt of dish washing liquid. Make a variety of clown colors. Let the children experiment with putting the clown paint on their faces but being careful to avoid their eyes. This face paint will clean up easily with soap and water.

Bubble Bath Paint

You will need: 2 cups flour   liquid bubble bath   spoon or utensil for stirring
1 teaspoon salt   food coloring   mixing bowls
water

What you do:
Combine the flour and salt with water until you have a paste. Add enough bubble bath to create a shampoo-like consistency. Then, add a few drops of food coloring. Your child will love to be able to paint himself; you will love that the paint will wash off the child, the walls, and the tub! Even though the water will become colored, no stains will be left on your child's skin.

Name: _____

Directions: Use bingo
markers to color the
gum balls.

Gum Ball Machine

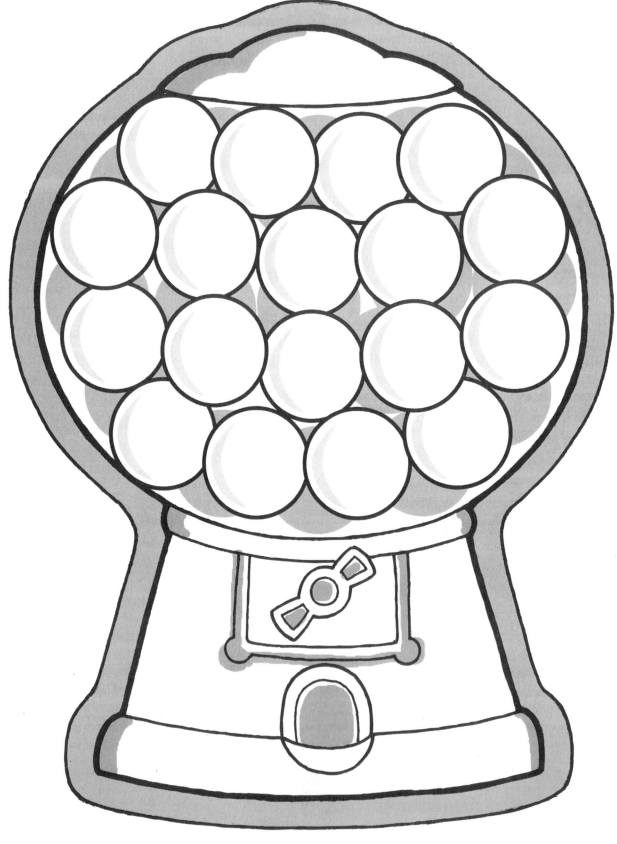

 **ART**

Directions: Paint the squirrel brown.

Squirrel

Name: _____

Directions: Paint the leaf green.

Leaf

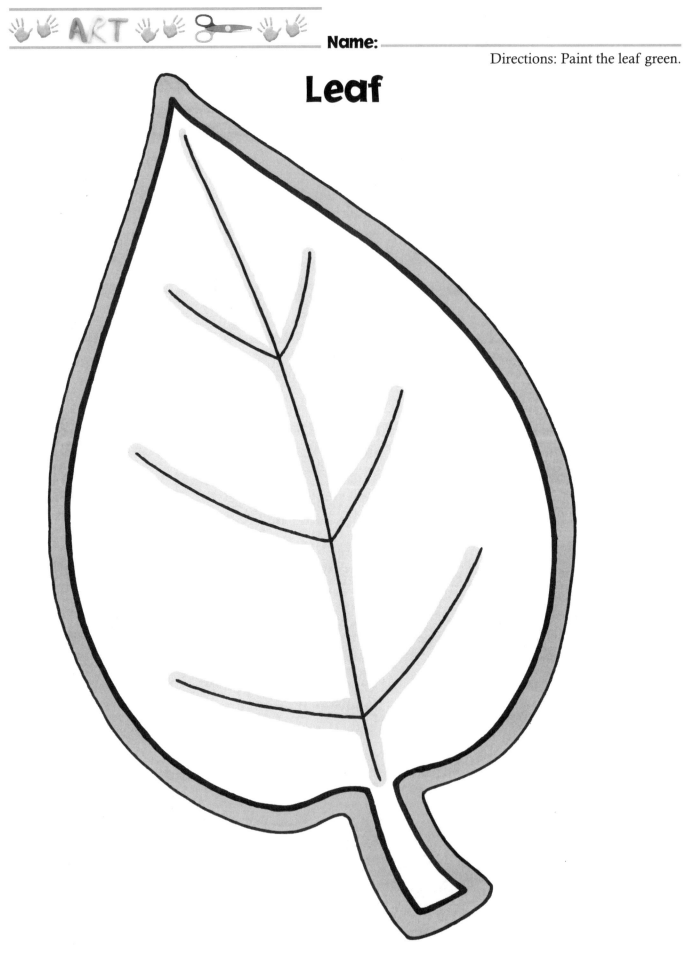

Directions: Paint the ghost gray.

Ghost

CRITICAL

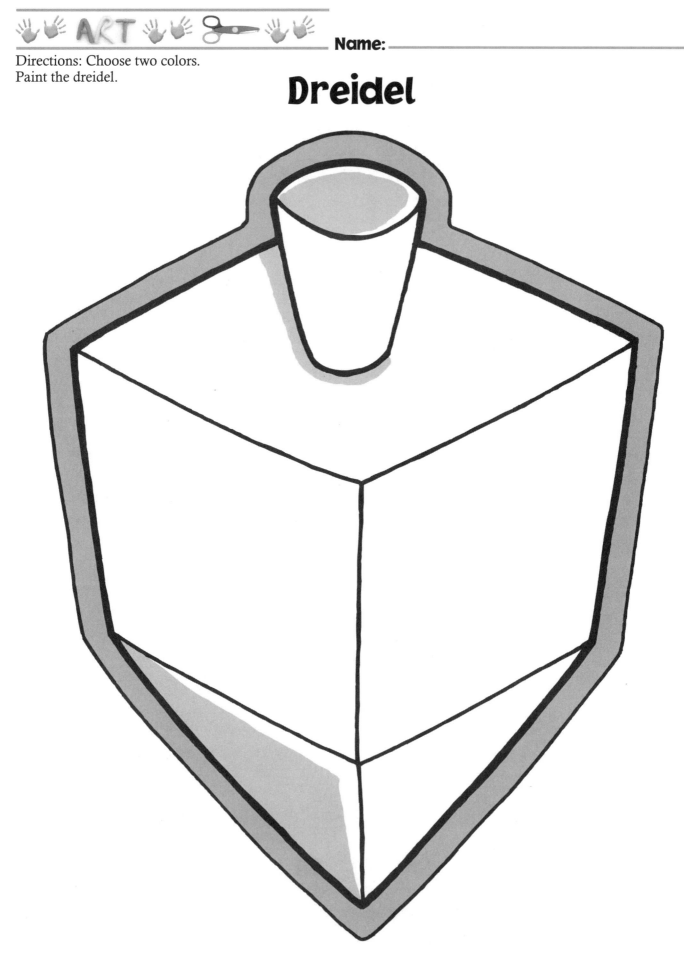

Directions: Choose two colors.
Paint the dreidel.

Dreidel

Name: _____

 **ART** ✂

Directions: Choose two colors.
Paint the gingerbread man.

Gingerbread Man

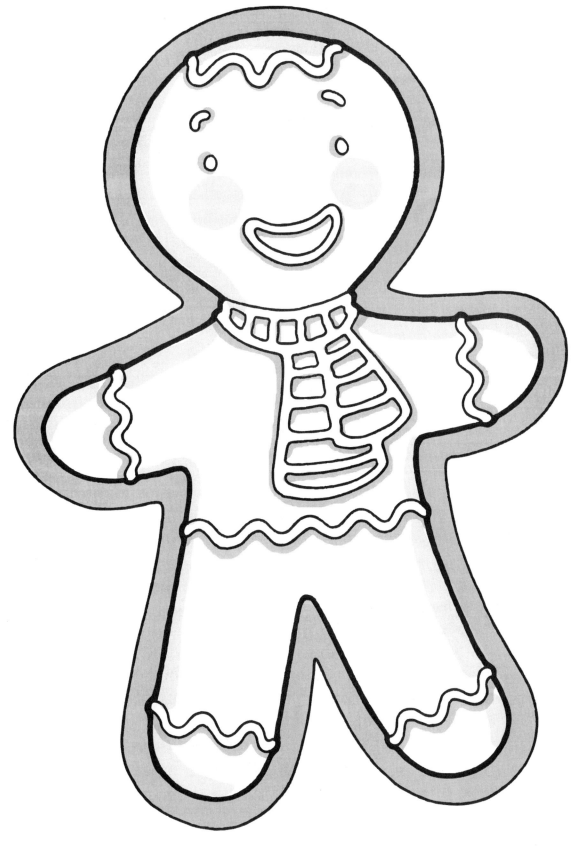

Name: _____

Heart

 **ART** Name: _____

Directions: Paint the sun yellow.
Paint the frog green.

Sun and Frog

Directions: Paint the bunny pink.

Name: _____

Bunny

 **ART**

Directions: Paint the lamb yellow.

Lamb

ART ✂

Directions: Choose two colors.
Paint the pail and shovel.

Pail & Shovel

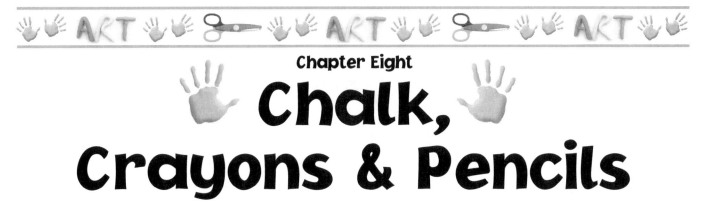

Chapter Eight

Chalk, Crayons & Pencils

Learning How to Hold a Pencil Properly

Some children just naturally know how to hold a pencil properly. But unfortunately, there are some children who struggle to learn this skill and must be taught proper pencil grasp. Below are some tips that will help you teach pencil skills.

• **Enable good posture.** Children should maintain good posture when they are learning how to print. Their feet should be on the floor and the desk surface should be at a height for their arms and elbows to rest comfortably. Ankles, hips, and knees should all be at 90 degree angles. If the chair is too high, place a footstool under the child's feet.

• **Provide a slanted surface.** Learning how to print is easier when children are permitted to work on a slanted surface. Place a four-inch three-ring binder on the desk in front of the child. The spine of the binder should be nearest the top of the desk. Rotate the binder to a 45-degree angle. Tape a piece of writing paper on the binder. Writing on this slanted surface is fun and can be extremely beneficial.

• **Align the writing paper.** Even if you do not use a slanted surface, be sure that the paper is aligned parallel to the arm of the child's dominant hand and is at a 45-degree angle. The nondominant hand should be used to hold the paper stable.

• **Promote proper pencil grasp.** The pencil should be held between the pads of the thumb and the index finger while resting on the middle finger. Another appropriate version of this grasp is for the pencil to be held between the pads of the thumb and the index and middle fingers while resting on the ring finger.

Extra Helpful Tips:

• **Use pencil grips.** Use pencil grips for children who have a difficult time remembering how to hold their pencils.

• **Provide short pencils.** Break or sharpen pencils down to about a two-inch length. This will encourage small hands to hold the pencil properly.

• **Try chubby writing tools.** Use sidewalk chalk, chubby crayons, or a chubby pencil shortened to a two-inch length to help children gain more control.

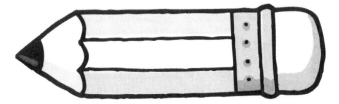

Make-Your-Own
Sidewalk Chalk Recipe

Big Sidewalk Chalk Sticks

You will need:
2 cups plaster of paris
2 cups cold water
toilet paper cardboard tubes
plastic mixing bowl
disposable stir sticks

tempera paint
duct tape
cookie sheet
waxed paper

What you do:

Cover the bottom of the cookie sheet with waxed paper. Use duct tape on one end of each toilet paper tube to seal it and set them on the cookie sheet with the taped side down. Pour the plaster of paris into the mixing bowl. Slowly add the water and blend it with a disposable stir stick. When the mixture resembles the texture of pudding, add the tempera paint.

Once the mixture is prepared, pour it into the toilet paper tubes. Gently tap the sides of the tubes to eliminate any air bubbles. Since these will be large chalk sticks, they will need two days to dry completely. After drying, tear off the cardboard tubes. Now, children can go outside and create!

Option: Help children to design their own sidewalk hopscotch games or to draw some fun mazes!

Caution: Be sure to read and follow all safety instructions on the plaster of paris label for chalk recipes on pages 78–79.

More Make-Your-Own Chalk Recipes

Little Sidewalk Chalk Sticks

You will need: 1 cup plaster of paris   plastic mixing bowl   tempera paint
1/2 cup cold water   disposable stir sticks   candy molds

What you do:

Pour the plaster of paris into the mixing bowl. Slowly add the water and stir with a disposable stir stick. When the mixture resembles the texture of pudding, add the tempera paint. Pour the mixture into the candy molds and let it dry completely—at least four hours. Pop the chalk out of the molds and have the children create some great drawings!

Rainbow Sidewalk Chalk

You will need: 2 cups plaster of paris   tempera paint   waxed paper
2 cups cold water   duct tape   disposable stir sticks
toilet paper cardboard tubes   cookie sheet   plastic mixing bowls

What you do:

Cover the bottom of the cookie sheet with waxed paper. Use duct tape on one end of each toilet paper tube to seal it and set them with the taped side down on the cookie sheet. Pour the plaster of paris into the mixing bowl. Slowly add the water and stir. Divide the plaster mixture into three or four bowls. Add a different color of tempera paint to each bowl. Layer the various colored plasters into the toilet paper tubes. Let them dry for two days and then remove the cardboard tubes to reveal the rainbow of colors!

Incredible Eggshell Chalk

You will need: 6 to 8 washed eggshells   1 teaspoon hot water   paper towel
1 teaspoon flour   food coloring

What you do:

Wash the eggshells and dry them completely. They should be free of any egg residue. Take them outside, or somewhere that you don't mind a mess, and grind the shells into a powder. (You may also grind them in a blender.) Remove any large shell pieces from the powder. In a small dish, mix the flour and eggshell powder. Then, add the teaspoon of very hot water and stir until it looks like a thick paste. You can add a drop or two of food coloring (or tempera paint) for color.

Roll the mixture into the shape of a chalk stick and wrap it in a paper towel or cloth. The incredible eggshell chalk will need approximately three days to dry.

Silly Spray "Chalk"

You will need: 4 tablespoons cornstarch   food coloring
1 cup warm water   spray bottles

What you do:

Mix the cornstarch and water in a bowl. Make sure that the cornstarch dissolves completely. Add food coloring to get the desired color. Pour the mixture into a spray bottle and shake it well. This spray will look like chalk after it dries. It can be sprayed on sand, snow, sidewalks, and paper.

Chalk Art Activities

Sensational Starch Chalk Art

You will need: water   mixing bowl   paintbrush
liquid starch   construction paper   colored chalk
spoon or utensil for stirring

What you do:

In a bowl, mix together equal parts of water and liquid starch. Have children brush the mixture all over pieces of construction paper. Then, they can draw on the wet paper with colored chalk. When the paper dries, the starch will act as a fixative, and the chalk will not smear.

Buttermilk Chalk Art

You will need: buttermilk   paintbrush
colored chalk   construction paper

What you do:

Brush the buttermilk over a piece of construction paper or manila paper, such as a plain file folder. Draw with colored chalk on the paper when it is still wet from the buttermilk. When dry, the drawing will have an interesting finish.

Sweet Water Chalk Art

You will need: water   spoon or utensil for stirring
sugar   colored chalk
plastic mixing bowl   construction paper

What you do:

Fill a bowl with water. Add several tablespoons of sugar and stir to dissolve it. Then, place the colored chalk in the water and let it soak for no more than five minutes. Invite children to draw with the wet chalk on the construction paper. When the chalk dries, it will have an interesting look.

Option: Try this activity without adding sugar to the water. Can the children see a difference?

Wet Paint Chalk Art

You will need: white liquid tempera paint   small bowl
colored chalk   construction paper

What you do:

Pour some white liquid tempera paint into a small bowl. Have the children dip the tip of the colored chalk into the white paint and draw on the construction paper. You can see the colors of the chalk through the paint, and the white edges created by the paint provide an interesting finish.

Option: Experiment with different colors of paint and with different colors of construction paper.

Color Crayon Recipes

Solid-Color Crayons

You will need: crayon pieces, paper removed   saucepan   muffin pan
empty tin can   baking cup paper liners   rack for cooling the pan
water   oven mitt or pot holder

What you do:
Place baking cup paper liners in the muffin pan. Add 2 1/2" of water to the saucepan. Pinch the top of the empty tin can to create a pouring spout. Fill the can one-quarter full of broken crayons of the same color. Set the can in the water. Over medium heat, bring the water to a boil. When the crayons have melted, carefully pour the melted crayon wax into the paper liners in the pan. Place the pan on a cooling rack and let the wax cool completely before removing the paper liners from the crayons.

Option 1: Try layering solid colors of melted crayon wax. Pour a small amount of the melted wax in the baking cup paper liners. Let it cool and add another color; then, add another color, and so on.

Option 2: Make new colors by melting together crayons of different colors. For example, melt red and yellow crayons and stir the colors together with a craft stick to create orange.

Swirly Rainbow Crayons

You will need: crayon pieces, paper removed
mini muffin pan
oven mitt or pot holder
rack for cooling the pan
craft stick (optional)

What you do:
Fill a mini muffin pan or a candy mold with small pieces of crayons. To make rainbow crayons, place four or five different colors of crayon pieces in each section. Place the pan in a 250°F oven just long enough for the crayons to melt. Watch carefully—crayon wax melts quickly! If you leave the crayons in the oven too long, the colors will blend together completely. The crayons should be soft—but not liquified. Take the pan out of the oven and place it on a cooling rack. Use a craft stick to swirl the colors a bit if desired. After the pan has cooled, pop out the crayons and let the children enjoy coloring!

Crayon Activities

Crayon Rubbings

You will need: color crayons, about 2" in length
paper
leaves from a variety of trees and plants

What you do:

Collect different types of leaves. Gather your old and broken pieces of crayon. Children will enjoy helping to remove the paper wrappers from crayon pieces. Have each child choose a leaf, lay it flat on a desktop, and place a piece of paper over it. By holding the crayon on its side and rubbing it over the paper, children can watch their leaves magically appear! They may wish to choose another leaf and crayon and repeat the process several times to create a collage of leaves on their papers.

Special tip: Place a piece of double-stick tape on the back of the leaf to help hold it in place while the child rubs over it with the crayon.

Option: Let children experiment with rubbing a variety of items: letters and numbers cut from card stock, seeds, coins, or any flat object with a texture.

Crayon Scratchings

You will need: color crayons   paintbrushes
white construction paper   plastic utensils
black tempera paint

What you do:

Give each child a piece of white construction paper and let her scribble all over the paper! Encourage children to press hard to create heavy color. When the crayon masterpieces are complete, have children paint over their entire pictures with black tempera paint. When the paint is still wet, let children scratch over their pictures with plastic utensils to reveal the colors underneath. Even though the utensils are plastic, this activity should still be supervised.

Melted Crayon Stained Glass

You will need: crayons, paper removed   iron
newspaper   ironing board
waxed paper   cloth or dish towel
pencil sharpener or cheese grater

What you do:

This project requires adult help and close supervision. Cover a table with newspaper and place a piece of waxed paper on the newspaper. Give the child a pencil sharpener or cheese grater. Let the child either carefully sharpen or grate many different colors of crayons onto the waxed paper. As soon as the child feels there are enough crayon shavings, place another piece of waxed paper over the shavings. Carefully pick up both pieces of waxed paper and place them on an ironing board. Then, cover the waxed paper with a cloth and lightly iron over the cloth. As the crayons melt, the colors will spread out over the waxed paper. Tape the waxed paper to a window so that sunlight will shine through the paper like stained glass.

More Crayon Activities

Chubby, Chubby Crayons

You will need:
- color crayons
- tape
- paper

What you do:

Tape several crayons together. This chubby, chubby crayon is easy for a young child to hold and creates several lines at once. Encourage children to experiment with drawing straight, wavy, and then looping lines. Talk about the shapes and patterns that emerge as lines are overlapped.

Option: Tape several different colors together to create "rainbow crayons."

Reproducible Fun Coloring Page Ideas

Here are some ideas for creative (and educational) ways to use pages 86–93. Each of these pages is designed for young children to add color to it.

Idea 1: Using white glue, trace around the edge of the picture and let it dry. This will provide a raised border, which makes it easier for children to color within the lines. Children can color in their pictures with crayons, markers, paint, or any medium of their choosing.

Idea 2: Glue yarn around the border of the picture. This will also provide a raised border to help guide the children's coloring.

Idea 3: After creating glue or yarn borders, let children fill in the rest of their pictures with colored glue. They can squeeze some glue into the center of the section they wish to color and then move the glue around with a cotton swab or a small paintbrush.

Idea 4: Give children bingo markers to fill in sections of color on any of the reproducible pages. The children can simply dab color in each section.

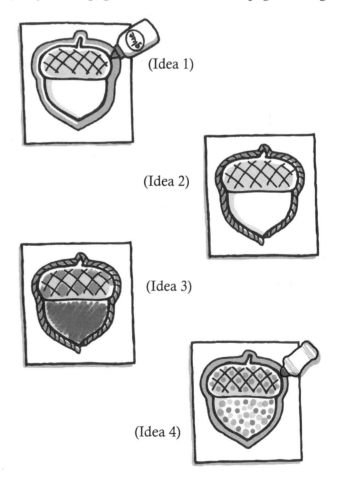

(Idea 1)

(Idea 2)

(Idea 3)

(Idea 4)

Stencils

Directions: Reproduce the stencil pattern on card stock. Carefully cut out the image. (Save the inside cutout to use for a variety of activities, such as crayon rubbings on page 82, collages on page 44, or, if decorated, stick puppets on page 37.) Begin by having the child hold the stencil securely with the nondominant hand while the dominant hand traces around the inside of the shape. You may aid very young children by using a few pieces of tape to help hold the stencil in place. Children will also enjoy dabbing paint with a sponge or large paintbrush or using a bingo marker to color inside the stencil's shape.

(Directions are found on page 84.)

Stencils (cont.)

Acorn

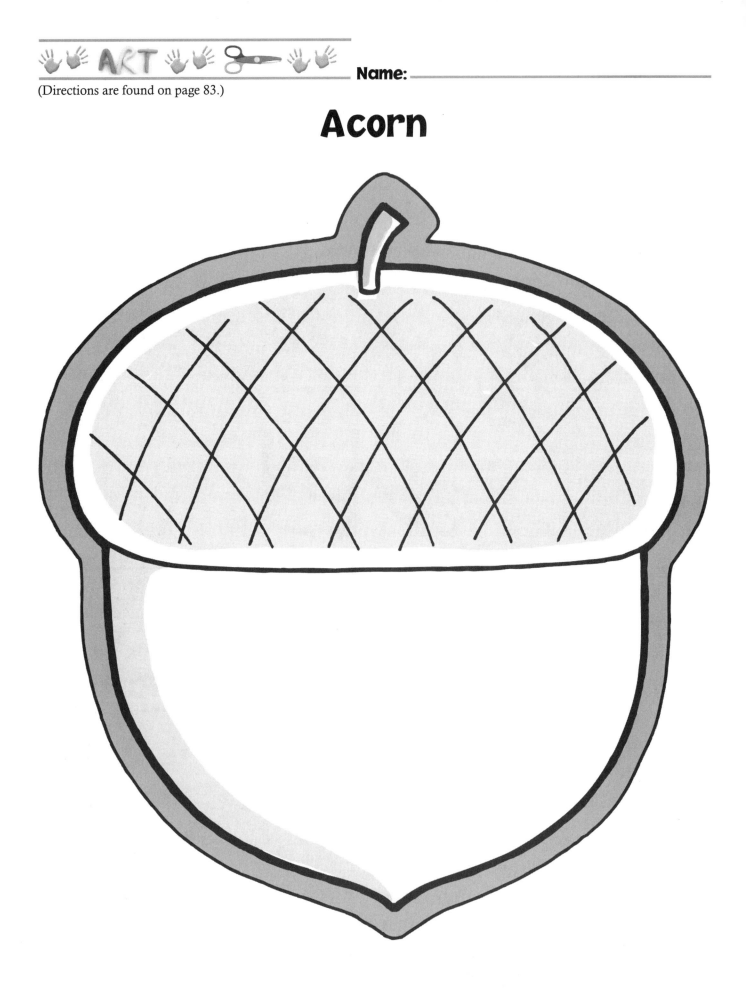

(Directions are found on page 83.)

Name: _____

Candy Corn

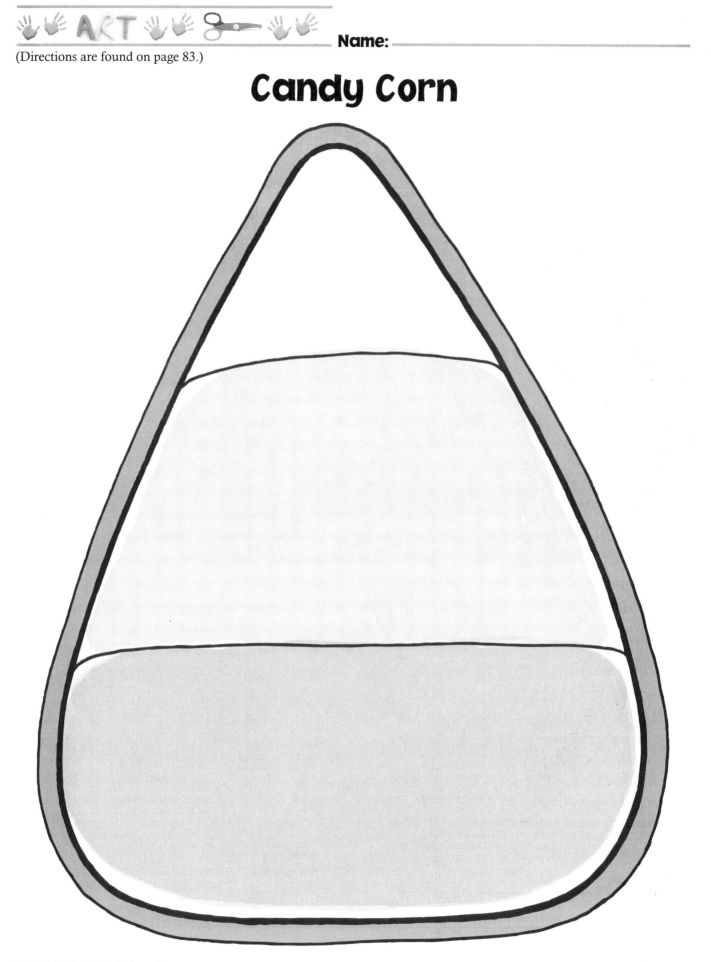

(Directions are found on page 83.)

Name: _____

Tepee

Ideas to Display Art

String It Along

Hang a length of clothesline, cording, ribbon, or rickrack. Attach the art to spring-type clothespins. Or, hang a curtain rod and the artwork can be displayed with clip rings or clamped into pants or skirt hangers.

Special tip: Using this method to showcase art has many advantages: the display is completely flexible for the size of work and number of pieces you wish to hang. Rotating pieces to keep the display fresh is quick and easy and it can be moved around the classroom to accommodate your needs.

Recycle Bakeware

Old cookie sheets, pizza pans, platters, and trays can serve as frames. Let children paint them with bright colors; hang them on a wall for a permanent display area or attach pieces of art and prop them up on bookshelves or ledges. You can also purchase inexpensive foil pans in a variety of sizes for an eye-catching arrangement.

Box It Up

Collect a variety of boxes; any size box or shape will work as long as it can be closed. Cover the boxes with contact paper or invite the children to paint them. Pictures can be taped on all sides—simply flip or turn the box to change the display.

Special tip: Attaching photo album pocket sheet protectors to the sides of the boxes will allow you to easily slide art in and out. This will also protect the art pieces as the boxes are rotated.

Wrap It Around

Large pieces of art can be wrapped around buckets or other storage containers. Cover the artwork with clear contact paper for protection. This makes a beautiful—and functional—display!

File a Frame

Create frames from manila or colorful file folders. Simply cut out a window in one side of each folder. This is a great solution to both display and store additional pieces of art. You can rotate pictures to the front, using removable double stick tape to "close" the frame after the artwork has been changed.

Correlations to the Standards

This book supports many domain element examples in The Head Start Child Development and Early Learning Framework and selected Achievement Standards in The National Standards for Art Education.

The Head Start Child Development and Early Learning Framework
U. S. Department of Health and Human Services,
Administration on Children, Youth and Families/Head Start Bureau.
The Head Start Child Development and Early Learning Framework. Washington, D.C.

Activities in this book support the following examples in the Head Start Child Outcomes Framework:

Physical Development & Health: Fine Motor Skills
• Develops hand strength and dexterity.
• Develops eye-hand coordination to use everyday tools, such as pitchers for pouring or utensils for eating.
• Manipulates a range of objects, such as blocks or books.
• Manipulates writing, drawing, and art tools.
Approaches to Learning: Initiative & Curiosity
• Demonstrates flexibility, imagination, and inventiveness in approaching tasks and activities.
Logic & Reasoning: Reasoning & Problem Solving
• Classifies, compares, and contrasts objects, events, and experiences.
Logic & Reasoning: Symbolic Representation
• Represents people, places, or things through drawings, movement, and three-dimensional objects.
Language Development: Receptive Language
• Attends to language during conversations, songs, stories, or other learning experiences.
Language Development: Expressive Language
• Engages in communication and conversation with others.
• Uses language to express ideas and needs.
• Engages in storytelling.
• Engages in conversations with peers and adults.
Literacy Knowledge & Skills: Alphabet Knowledge
• Recognizes that the letters of the alphabet are a special category of visual graphics that can be individually named.
Literacy Knowledge & Skills: Print Concepts & Conventions
• Recognizes print in everyday life, such as numbers, letters, one's name, words, and familiar logos and signs.
Literacy Knowledge & Skills: Early Writing
• Experiments with writing tools and materials.
• Uses scribbles, shapes, pictures, and letters to represent objects, stories, experiences, or ideas.
Creative Arts Expression: Music
• Participates in music activities, such as listening, singing, or performing.
Creative Arts Expression: Art
• Uses different materials and techniques to make art creations.
• Creates artistic works that reflect thoughts, feeling, experiences, or knowledge.
• Discusses one's own artistic creations and those of others.

National Standards for Arts Education

All bolded text below: From *National Standards for Arts Education*. Copyright © 1994 by Music Educators National Conference (MENC). Used by permission. The complete National Arts Standards and additional materials relating to the Standards are available from MENC: The National Association for Music Education, 1806 Robert Fulton Drive, Reston, VA 20191; www.menc.org.

This book supports the following visual arts content and achievement standards for K-4 students from the National Standards for Arts Education:
Content Standard 1: Understanding and applying media, techniques, and processes

Achievement Standards:
Students know the differences between materials, techniques, and processes. Students use a wide variety of materials and techniques to do the art activities in *Fine Motor Projects*.

Students use different media, techniques, and processes to communicate ideas, experiences, and stories. Students use a variety of materials and techniques to communicate ideas in their art projects.

Students use art materials and tools in a safe and responsible manner. *Fine Motor Projects* emphasizes the safe use of all art materials.

Chapter Nine

Ideas to Display Art

Classroom Tips: Encourage, Inspire & Celebrate

Now that your artists have created a variety of masterpieces, there are many imaginative ways to spotlight their work. On these two pages, you'll find plenty of creative solutions for showcasing children's art projects. For even more fun and fine motor skill practice, many of these display ideas can be decorated by the children as well! And, by setting aside special "art gallery" spaces, you will show children that their efforts are valued and will encourage even more artistic expression.

Special tip: Change the pictures in the displays regularly and often to keep children's interest.

Create class big books

Combine paintings and drawings in scrapbooks or slip them into large photo album sleeves. Have children decorate card stock to create covers for the books. Punch holes as needed and use loose leaf binder rings or tie with yarn. Children will love to page through their work.

Special tip: Be sure artists have signed their names to their pieces of art. You can also write short descriptions of their artwork if appropriate.

Make picture place mats

Laminate large pieces of artwork and use them as place mats for snack time or anytime a surface needs protection from a fun—and messy—activity. You can simply wipe off the mats and leave them out where they can be seen.

Paint the edges

For an easy-to-do finished look, simply paint each edge of the artwork black, brown, or any color that complements the piece. You can also use strips of colored tape or pieces of fabric to create the look of a frame.

Frame it with imagination

Use different sizes of cardboard and cut out windows to frame the art. Let children decorate the cardboard frames with paint; they can glue on objects such as shells, colored pasta, buttons, tissue paper squares, stickers, and glitter. They can also add texture to their frames with glue, pieces of fabric, and sponges and splatters of puff paint.

Set out the sculptures

In a low-traffic area, try a combination of window ledges, boxes, bookshelves, and plant stands to create a corner for 3-D art pieces.

Canadian Flag

(Directions are found on page 83.)

US Flag

Basket with Flowers

Name: _____

Fine Motor Projects

Duckling

Name:

Kite

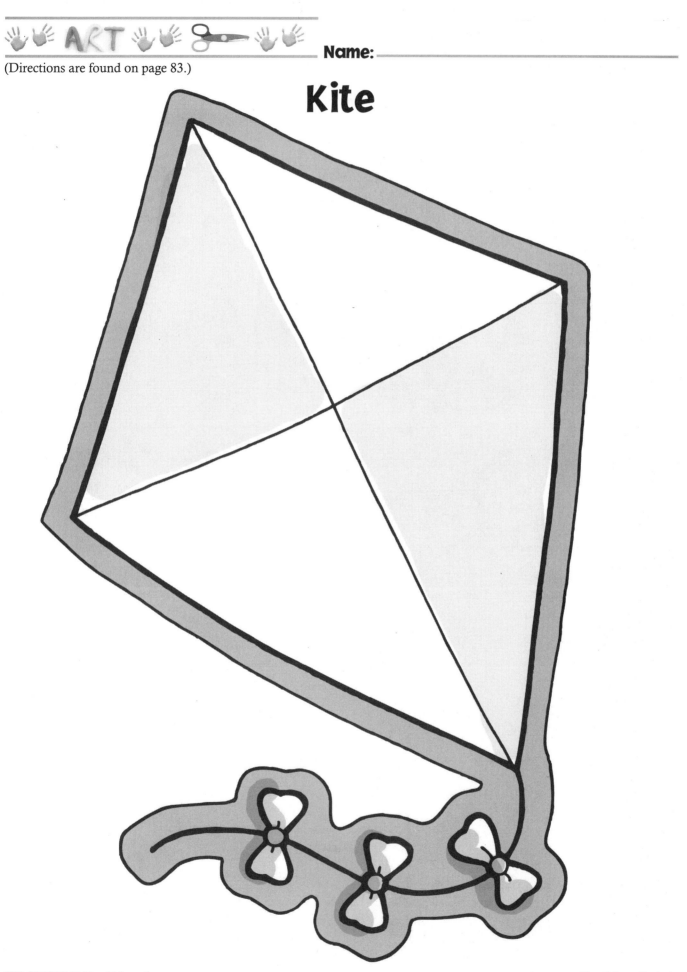